Scarves
and Shawls
for Yarn Lovers

Scarves
and Shawls
for Yarn Lovers

KNITTING WITH SIMPLE PATTERNS
AND AMAZING YARNS

Carri Hammett

Creative Publishing
international

Chanhassen, MN

Creative Publishing international

Copyright 2006
Creative Publishing international
18705 Lake Drive East
Chanhassen, Minnesota 55317
1-800-328-3895
www.creativepub.com
All rights reserved

President/CEO: Ken Fund
Executive Editor: Alison Brown Cerier
Executive Managing Editor: Barbara Harold
Senior Editor: Linda Neubauer
Photo Stylist: Joanne Wawra
Creative Director: Brad Springer
Photo Art Director: Tim Himsel
Photographers: Steve Galvin, Andrea Rugg,
    Joel Schnell
Production Manager: Laura Hokkanen
Book Design: Lois Stanfield

Acknowledgments

So many people have inspired me and helped me to write this book. I owe my thanks to my employees who had the patience of saints, to my customers and friends who inspired me with their ideas and creativity, and to my teachers who so generously shared their knowledge.

Most especially I want to thank my family members who give their love so freely. Your tolerance and humor, as always, have kept me going, and I promise I will clean the house someday. REALLY!

Library of Congress Cataloging-in-Publication Data

Hammett, Carri.
    Scarves and shawls for yarn lovers : knitting with simple patterns and amazing yarns /
Carri Hammett.
        p. cm.
ISBN-13: 978-1-58923-257-0 (soft cover)
    ISBN-10: 1-58923-257-7 (soft cover)
1. Knitting--Patterns. 2. Scarves. 3. Shawls.
I. Title.
    TT825.H2565 2006
    746.43'20432--dc22   2006002493

Printed in China
10 9 8 7 6 5 4 3 2

For any of the fabulous yarns used in these projects, or to make inspired choices of your own, visit Carri's shop or Web site:
Coldwater Collaborative
347 Water Street
Excelsior, MN 55331
www.coldwateryarn.com

Also check these yarn company Web sites:
Alchemy Yarns - www.alchemyyarns.com
Berroco - www.berroco.com
Blue Heron Yarns - www.blueheronyarns.com
Blue Sky Alpacas - www.blueskyalpacas.com
Caron - www.caron.com
Classic Elite Yarns - www.classiceliteyarns.com
Colinette - www.uniquekolours.com
Crystal Palace - www.crystalpalaceyarns.com
Di.ve' - www.cascadeyarn.com
Fiesta Yarns - www.fiestayarns.com
Filati FF - www.knittingfever.com
Filatura di Crosa - www.tahkistacycharles.com
Great Adirondack Yarn - www.yarnrep.com
Habu Textiles - www.habutextiles.com
Ironstone Yarns - www.yarnrep.com
Katia - www.knittingfever.com
Laines du Nord - www.knittingfever.com
Lana Grossa - www.lanagrossa.de
Lion Brand - www.lionbrand.com
Madil Yarns - www.cascadeyarn.com
Manos del Uruguay - Design Source 888-566-9970
Moda Dea - www.modadea.com
Muench Yarns/GGH - www.muenchyarns.com
Nashua Handknits - www.westminsterfibers.com
On Line - www.knittingfever.com
Plymouth - www.plymouthyarn.com
Queensland Collection - www.knittingfever.com
S. Charles Collezione - www.tahkistacycharles.com
South West Trading Company - www.soysilk.com
Trendsetter - www.trendsetteryarns.com
Wool in the Woods - www.woolinthewoods.com

Contents

For the Love of Yarn

Carri Hammett is the owner of Coldwater Collaborative, a gem of a yarn shop in Excelsior, Minnesota. Forever a fiber fiend, Carri uses her creativity and strong color sense in weaving, quilting, and, of course, knitting. She loves to teach people about knitting and really enjoys helping customers with challenging projects. Carri lives in Minnesota with her husband, two of her three kids, and a dog with whom she has a love-hate relationship.

When customers come into my shop, they are often dazzled by the yarns. The space is full of textures and colors in endless variety. There are solid, self-striping, variegated, and hand-dyed yarns. There are classic yarns, luxury yarns, and novelty yarns—wool, silk, cashmere, ribbon, eyelash, and chenille.

Yarns today are amazing, but all those choices can feel overwhelming. As a shop owner, it's my job to help customers make their selections. I tell them there is no single choice for any project, but there are definitely good and even better choices. The right choice will be a yarn that you absolutely love, and that your project will show off to its best advantage.

While many books and patterns focus on complicated stitch patterns, I've found that simple stitches often show off fabulous yarns better. Certain stitches will enhance the beauty of certain fibers especially well. For example, seed stitch is an excellent choice for ribbon yarn because it allows more of the ribbon to be seen. A complicated stitch isn't worth the effort when working with highly textured yarn since the pattern won't be seen anyway.

For exploring new yarns, scarves and shawls are ideal projects. Scarves are simple by nature, with no worries about fit or sizing. You've probably already made one scarf—or dozens—so you can concentrate on the yarn instead of learning lots of new techniques. Scarves are small-scale projects, too, so you can try a new stitch or a new yarn without investing a lot of your time or money. Speaking of money, a scarf takes less yarn than a sweater or throw, so go ahead and try that luxury yarn you've been worshipping.

I've designed twenty scarves and shawls that match a wonderful yarn or combination of yarns with a simple design. I'll share why I think the match is a good one so you can enhance your own knitting knowledge. For each project, I've also designed a variation with the same stitch pattern and very different yarn. The difference the yarn makes is fascinating and often dramatic.

ABOUT THE PROJECTS

The book starts with the simplest stitch pattern, then introduces new techniques with each project, often building on skills introduced earlier. Nothing is difficult—even a beginner can knit anything in the book.

If you're a new knitter, you will find it easiest to start at the beginning of the book and knit your way through it. If a particular project doesn't appeal to you, I suggest you read through the directions anyway and practice the techniques with scrap yarns. For a review of basic stitches, go to Knitting 101 in the back of the book. If you are a more experienced knitter, you can make the scarves in any order.

When a project introduces a technique or stitch pattern that is new to you, go to the Knitting Class in that project for step-by-step instructions and photographs. The Knitting Class topics are:
Two Yarns Together (pg. 18)
Parking and Picking Up (pg. 28)
Beaded Fringe (pg. 29)
Customized Fringe (pg. 42)
Striping (pg. 48)
Twisted Drop Stitch (pg. 58)
Stripes with Odd Numbers of Rows (pg. 76)
Casting On Big Time (pg. 83)
Drop Stitch (pg. 92)

I've also included my favorite Knit Tips to make your knitting experience more relaxing and enjoyable. Many of the tips are answers to the questions my customers have asked me when they're learning to knit.

Each project includes generic descriptions of the yarns used as well as the specific brand and color and amounts to buy if you want to copy the design exactly. By following the generic descriptions, you can substitute other yarns with similar characteristics. I've also included a variation swatch of each design, knitted in the same stitch pattern but with different yarns to show you the tip of this iceberg of possibilities that awaits you. For each variation, you'll find the name brands and colors of the yarns used, the needles, and gauge along with an estimate of the yarn amounts needed. Buy extra yarn, if you are unsure.

IT'S ALL ABOUT THE YARN

To make the most of this exciting needle art, explore knitting with as many different types of yarn as possible. It is so much fun to use the same basic shape, such as a scarf, to explore many different textures.

When you go shopping, purchase the best yarn you can afford. I'm not saying this because I own a yarn shop. You are far more likely to finish your projects when you invest in high-quality yarn that you adore. If you compromise on a low-quality yarn or one that doesn't make your heart beat a little faster, then you won't love knitting with it.

Here is a basic introduction to the yarns used in the book. The numbers refer to the photo on page 8.

Smooth yarn (1), or plied, has an even texture and the same thickness throughout. It is made from either a single ply or several plies twisted together, and can be made of animal (wool, alpaca, cashmere), plant (silk, bamboo, rayon, cotton), or synthetic (acrylic, polyester, nylon) fibers.

Mohair (2) is a lightweight, fuzzy yarn that is spun from the fleece of Angora goats. Nylon and/or wool are usually added to help the fibers cling together.

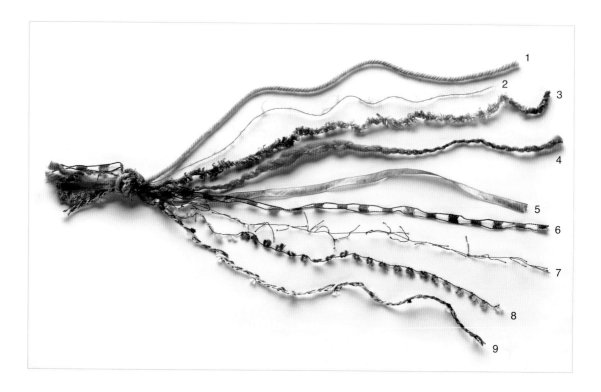

Chenille (3) is very soft and it is usually made from rayon or cotton. It has a short, velvety pile that is locked in by a thin, strong core.

Slub, nub, and bouclé yarns have an uneven texture (4). Each is technically different, but with so many yarns being produced, the distinctions have blurred. When different fibers are spun at different tension, the resulting yarn can be thick and thin, have loops held in place by a binder yarn, or have bumps at intervals along a plied yarn. Sometimes the yarns have all three!

Ribbon yarn (5) is available in a wide range of widths and fibers. It is either woven on a modified loom or knitted like a miniature stocking. The texture varies from soft and supple to crinkled and crisp.

Ladder yarn (6) is made of two side-by-side base fibers that are connected at intervals by strands of yarn that form the steps of the ladder. The space between the steps and the thickness and density of the steps vary. Sometimes a second fiber is twined between the steps.

Eyelash and fur yarns (7) are composed of multiple strands of fiber that protrude from a central chained core yarn. The strands can either be woven in at intervals or continuously. Depending on the density and length of the strand, the yarn is known as eyelash or fur.

Novelty and component yarns (8) are often used in combination with heavier, stronger yarns. A thin central core yarn is woven so that "flags" of fiber stick out at regular intervals. The knitted effect is more or less dense depending on the closeness of the flags.

Multi-fiber yarn (9) combines any of the above. Component yarn might be combined with bouclé or mohair. Some yarns have three or even four different fibers.

WHAT'S IN YOUR BAG?

Knitting doesn't require a lot of expensive supplies. At first, all you need is yarn, knitting needles, scissors, and a blunt-end yarn needle. I also recommend a sturdy bag or basket that will hold your knitting and keep small children, Fido, and Fluffy out. (Dogs are great for my business because they love to chew bamboo knitting needles, and everyone knows what a cat will do to a ball of yarn!)

Knitting needles

Knitting needles are made from a variety of materials. I prefer bamboo needles because they are lightweight, warm to the touch, and smooth without being slippery (good for new knitters). Unlike metal needles, bamboo needles don't click, which means you can knit in bed without disturbing anyone, if you know what I mean.

There are three types of needles: straight, double-pointed, and circular. Only straight and circular needles are used in this book. Straight needles are generally available in two lengths and are sold in pairs. I like to use the shortest needle possible that will fit the number of stitches required by the pattern; I usually use a 9" (23 cm) pair. Circular needles are basically two short, straight needles that are connected by a flexible cable. You can use a circular needle to knit back and forth (instead of in the round) when your pattern has so many stitches that they won't fit on a straight needle. I usually use a 24" (61 cm) circular needle.

Needles are sized according to the diameter of the shaft, with larger numbers indicating bigger needles. Sizes are given in both US standard numbers (for example, size 9) and metric (for example, 5.5 mm); the most common sizes range from size 1 to size 19 (2.25 to 15 mm).

Blunt-end yarn needle

A blunt-end yarn needle, also called a tapestry needle, is a metal or plastic hand-sewing needle with a large eye and a blunt tip. It is used for weaving in the leftover tails on your knitting. The large eye is essential to thread bulky yarns and the blunt tip glides around the stitches instead of piercing the yarn.

Other useful items

A tape measure is handy for checking your gauge and measuring your work. There are lots of small, retractable styles. A couple of crochet hooks in different sizes can be used for attaching fringe. Size J or K usually works well. Rubber point protectors can be placed on the tips of your needles to protect the points from damage—and to keep your knitting from slipping off. Ziplock plastic bags are great for holding your yarn while you knit and preventing tangles. Place a small notebook in your knitting bag for jotting down important information about your projects, like which row you stopped on or how many balls of yarn you need for your next project. A small knitting reference book is a must. (You'll learn everything you need for these projects here, though.)

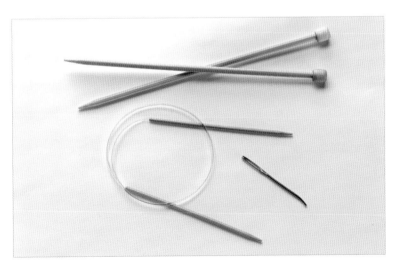

Simple Luxury

HAND-DYED CASHMERE IN GARTER STITCH

Garter stitch is the easiest stitch. You just knit every row. Though simple, garter stitch is a wonderful way to show off textured yarns. Garter stitch will not roll at the edges, but it does tend to stretch in length, so keep this in mind when you plan a scarf. The scarf shown here is knit from one of the most luxurious yarns: hand-dyed cashmere. One hank is enough to make this short, neck-hugging style, fastened with a classy scarf pin.

KNIT TIPS

You can use the garter stitch to explore how a particular yarn will look when knit with different sizes of needles. Cast on 10 or more stitches with the needle size recommended on the yarn label and knit a few inches. Switch to larger needles and knit a few inches more. Switch again to even larger needles. When you use really large needles in proportion to the weight of the yarn, you create a lacy texture, and the garter stitch ridges are not so obvious.

Medium-weight, smooth yarn: 70 yd (64 m)

Shown: Fiesta Yarns Lusso, 12 ply; *100% cashmere; 70 yd (64 m)/2 oz (57 g): 1 hank color #9135, Wild Oak*

NEEDLES AND NOTIONS

Size 13 (9 mm) needles or size needed to obtain gauge

Blunt-end yarn needle

GAUGE

11 stitches = 4" (10 cm) in garter stitch

FINISHED SIZE

3½" × 31" (9 × 78.5 cm)

SCARF

Cast on 10 stitches.

Row 1: Knit each stitch to end of row.

Repeat row 1 until yarn is almost gone, saving about 1 yd (0.91 m) to bind off. Bind off loosely.

FINISHING

1. Weave in all ends, using the blunt-end yarn needle.
2. Steam very lightly to block, if desired (page 111).

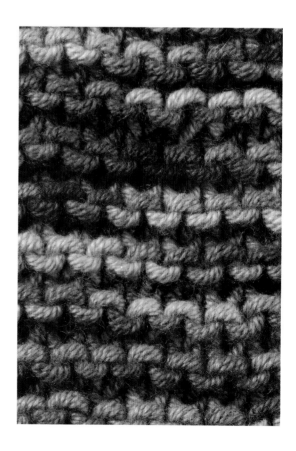

Same Colors, Different Texture

Garter stitch, because of its simplicity, is a good choice for knitting yarns with lots of textural interest. This bouclé (bumpy) yarn is the same color as the smooth yarn in the scarf on page 12 but is richly textured. Knit the bouclé yarn scarf with the same amount of yarn and the same size needles as the smooth yarn scarf, but since bouclé is a heavier yarn, cast on just 8 stitches for a scarf of the same width.

YARN

Bulky-weight bouclé yarn
Shown: Fiesta Yarns Tenero; *84% cashmere, 12% merino wool, 4% nylon; 70 yd (64 m)/2 oz (57 g): color #16135, Wild Oak*

NEEDLES

Size 13 (9 mm) needles or size needed to obtain gauge

GAUGE

9 stitches = 4" (10 cm) in garter stitch

Togetherness

TWO YARNS KNITTED AS ONE

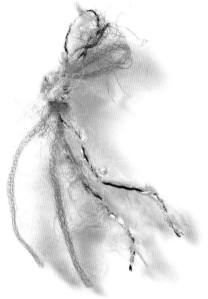

One of my favorite things to do with yarns is combine them. You can create fantastic effects when you mix yarns with each other. I often knit with two yarns at the same time; sometimes I knit with three or more. Choose yarns that don't match too closely in color or texture. Actually, the most effective combinations "fight" each other a little bit. If the colors are a little bit "off" before combining, then the finished appearance of the knitted item will be much more interesting.

KNIT TIPS

Tangled yarn can become a big problem when you are knitting with two or more balls. One of my favorite tricks is to put each ball into its own ziplock plastic bag. Snip off one corner and feed the end of the yarn through.

YARN

 Medium-weight bouclé and fur yarn (A): 155 yd (142 m)
Shown: On Line Linie 43 Punta; *45% rayon, 45% nylon, 10% acrylic; 87 yd (80 m)/1.75 oz (50 g): 2 balls color #30*

 Medium-weight kid mohair (B): 151 yd (138 m)
Shown: Muench Yarns/GGH Soft-Kid; *70% super kid mohair, 25% nylon, 5% wool; 151 yd (138 m)/0.875 oz (25 g): 1 ball color #013*

Hand-dyed silk ribbon, 7/16" (1.2 cm) wide: 5½ yd (5 m)
Shown: Artemis Hand Dyed Silk Ribbon; 5½ yd (5 m); color Solstice Sky

NEEDLES AND NOTIONS

Size 11 (8 mm) needles or size needed to obtain gauge

Blunt-end yarn needle

8/H (5 mm) crochet hook

GAUGE

12 stitches = 4" (10 cm) in garter stitch

FINISHED SIZE

45" × 6½" (114 × 16.5 cm), not including fringe

SCARF

With yarn A and yarn B held together, cast on 20 stitches. If this is a new technique for you, go to Knitting Class on page 18.

Row 1: With yarn A and yarn B held together, knit each stitch to end of row.

Repeat row 1 until the scarf is the desired length or until yarn B is almost gone, leaving about 1 yd (0.91 m) to bind off. Bind off loosely with yarn A and yarn B held together. You will need to start a new ball of yarn A midway through the scarf. If this technique is new to you, go to Knitting Class on page 18.

FINISHING

Using the blunt-end yarn needle, weave in all ends. It is not necessary to block this scarf.

FRINGE

1. Each fringe section will consist of two strands of yarn A. Every other fringe will also include a piece of silk ribbon.
2. Cut 52 pieces of yarn A, each 14" (36 cm) long.
3. Cut 14 pieces of silk ribbon, each 14" (36 cm) long.
4. Using a crochet hook and two strands of yarn A, space 13 fringes evenly across the bottom of the scarf. Starting with the first fringe, add a strand of silk ribbon to every other fringe. Repeat at the other end.

Different Textures·

This variation uses two yarns that are dyed the same color but have different textures. The result is a beautifully dense scarf that looks and feels luxurious. The scarf takes one ball of smooth yarn and two balls of the ladder yarn. The fringe is made using just the ladder yarn. Use the same size needles but only cast on 12 stitches and knit until yarn A is gone. Use the leftover yarn B for the fringe.

YARN

 Medium-weight smooth yarn (A)
Shown: Trendsetter Yarns Murano; *100% nylon; 60 yd (55 m)/0.875 oz (25 g): color #38*

 Medium-weight ladder yarn (B)
Shown: Trendsetter Yarns Sunshine; *75% rayon, 25% nylon; 95 yd (87 m)/1.75 oz (50 g); color #38*

NEEDLES

Size 11 (8 mm) needles or size needed to obtain gauge

GAUGE

14 stitches = 4" (10 cm) in garter stitch

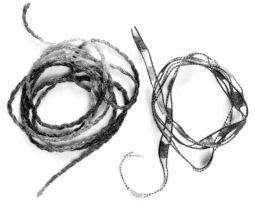

Two Yarns Together

Knitting while holding two yarns together might sound scary, but it's really very simple. Lots of patterns call for this technique, but it's rarely explained. Here's how to get started.

1. From each ball of yarn, pull out enough length to cast on the desired stitches; for a scarf, that's usually about 1 yard (0.91 m).

2. Line up the ends of the yarns and then run your fingers along the yarns together so they cling to each other (just for this beginning length—not the whole ball!).

3. Pinch the two yarns together where you plan to put your slipknot, and form the knot with both yarns as if they are one. Your "yarn" now consists of one strand each of two different yarns.

3

4. Now cast on and begin to knit, always using both strands of yarn together, treating them as if they were one strand. Each time the tip of the right needle enters a stitch on the left needle, it needs to go through both strands. Likewise, when you wrap the yarn over the right needle to complete a new stitch, you wrap both strands together.

You will usually be combining yarns that come from balls of different lengths, so you will run out of one strand before the other. For best results, plan ahead and change to the new ball at the beginning of a new row, leaving a tail at least 8" (20 cm) long from both the old ball and the new ball. Simply stop knitting with the old ball at the end of the row and start the new ball at the beginning of the next row, combining it with the other yarn as you continue knitting. When you finish the scarf, weave in these tails (page 109) just like those at the beginning and end of the scarf.

4

Sophisticated Glitz

LADDER YARN IN SEED STITCH

The seed stitch is one of my favorite stitches for a scarf. Alternating knit and purl stitches makes a scarf that is completely reversible and lies perfectly flat. Seed stitch is ideal for ribbon yarn because it allows a lot of the surface of the ribbon to be seen. Used with this novelty ladder yarn, the seed stitch creates a pleasing granular texture that's a wonderful counterpoint to the glitzy character of the yarn. A coordinating ladder yarn that drapes beautifully is used for the fringe.

KNIT TIPS

Cast on an odd number of stitches for seed-stitch scarves. That way, every row begins and ends with a knit stitch and you don't have to worry about what side you are on.

. . . .

Learn to recognize what stitches look like on your needle. A knit stitch forms a smooth V right under the needle and a bump on the opposite side. A purl stitch forms a bump right under the needle and smooth V on the opposite side. In seed stitch, you do the opposite of what the stitch looks like. If you see a bump right under the needle, then knit the stitch; if you see a V, then purl the stitch.

YARN

 Bulky-weight ladder/bouclé yarn (A): 120 yd (110 m)
Shown: Plymouth Odyssey Glitz; *60% nylon, 37% wool, 3% lamé; 65 yd (59 m)/1.75 oz (50 g): 2 balls color #117*

 Medium-weight ladder yarn (B): 17 yd (15.5 m)
Shown: Plymouth Eros Glitz; *86% rayon, 10% nylon, 4% Lurex; 158 yd (145 m)/1.75 oz (50 g): 1 ball color #117*

NEEDLES AND NOTIONS

Size 11 (8 mm) needles or size needed to obtain gauge

Blunt-end yarn needle

Size 8/H (5 mm) crochet hook

GAUGE

10 stitches = 4" (10 cm) in seed stitch

FINISHED SIZE

5" × 45" (12.7 × 115 cm), not including fringe

SCARF

Using yarn A, cast on 13 stitches.

Row 1: * Knit 1, purl 1 *, repeat from * to * until 1 stitch remains, end with knit 1.

Remember to bring the yarn back and forth between the needles as you switch between knit and purl.

Repeat row 1 until scarf is desired length or until yarn is almost gone, leaving about 1 yd (0.91 m) to bind off. Bind off loosely.

FINISHING

Using the blunt-end yarn needle, weave in all ends. Wet block (page 111) the scarf, if desired.

FRINGE

1. Cut 40 pieces of yarn B, each 15" (38 cm) long.
2. Using two pieces of yarn B per fringe, evenly space 10 fringes along each short edge.
3. Trim the ends of all the yarns to even up the length, if desired.

Soft and Simple

This variation is made with the same number of stitches using the same size needle. Can you believe how different it looks? This lovely alpaca yarn is enhanced by the rhythmic quality of the seed-stitch pattern. You will need 100 yards (91 m) to make a waist-length scarf; you may want to make it longer to wrap around your neck since it's so warm and soft. Plan to use at least 150 to 200 yards (137 to 183 m) to make a long scarf. Attach a fringe, if you wish, but I like it unadorned—it's simple yet elegant.

YARN

 Bulky-weight smooth yarn
Shown: Plymouth Alpaca Grande; *100% baby alpaca; 109 yd (100 m)/3.5 oz (100 g): color #3317*

NEEDLES

Size 11 (8 mm) needles or size needed to obtain gauge

GAUGE

12 stitches = 4" (10 cm) in seed stitch

A Wink of Eyelash

RIBBON YARN STRIPED WITH EYELASH

The key to using eyelash effectively is moderation. Just a little bit adds texture and enhances the scarf, but if you use too much eyelash, you can't see the companion yarn at all. For this scarf, you'll learn how to stripe the eyelash—use it on some rows but not on others. Not only does this technique enhance the beauty of your scarf, it stretches your wallet because you only need half as much eyelash yarn as the main yarn in your scarf. A simple seed-stitch pattern was used. Also notice the beads that have been added to the fringe. Eyelash doesn't work well for fringe, but the color of the beads continues the lavender accent from the scarf into the fringe.

KNIT TIPS

When fixing tangled eyelash, easy does it. If you pull too tightly or quickly on a tangle, you'll only make it worse. Gently tease out the yarn and pull on the tangle to keep it loose. Be nice to your eyelash!

YARN

 Bulky-weight ribbon yarn (A):
125 yd (114 m)
*Shown: Laines du Nord Ombre;
100% nylon; 74 yd (68 m)/1.75 oz
(50 g): 2 balls color #54*

Eyelash yarn (B): 63 yd (58 m)
*Shown: Trendsetter Yarns Eyelash;
100% polyester; 73 yd (67 m)/0.7oz
(20 g): 1 ball color #15*

NEEDLES AND NOTIONS

Size 13 (9 mm) needles or size
needed to obtain gauge

Blunt-end yarn needle

Crochet hook

Beading needle

Nylon beading thread

Seed beads, size 9°, about 45 g

GAUGE

11 stitches = 4" (10 cm) in seed stitch

FINISHED SIZE

4¾" x 48" (12 x 122 cm), not
including fringe

SCARF

With yarn A and yarn B held together, cast on 15 stitches.

Row 1: With yarn A and yarn B together, * knit 1, purl 1 *, repeat from * to * until 1 stitch remains, end with knit 1.

Row 2: Repeat row 1.

Row 3: Drop yarn B. With yarn A alone, * knit 1, purl 1 *, repeat from * to * until 1 stitch remains, end with knit 1.

Row 4: Repeat row 3.

Repeat rows 1 to 4 until the scarf is almost the desired length. Finish by repeating just rows 1 and 2. Bind off loosely with yarn A and yarn B held together.

If this striping technique has you a little confused, go to Knitting Class on page 28.

FINISHING

Using the blunt-end yarn needle, weave in all ends. It is not necessary to block this scarf.

FRINGE

1. Cut 14 pieces of ribbon yarn (A), each 13" (33 cm) long.
2. Using a crochet hook and one strand of ribbon yarn, space seven fringes evenly across each end of the scarf.
3. In the spaces between the ribbon fringes, complete six bead fringes. To add interest, use a larger bead at the end of each fringe and also vary the length.

Not familiar with beading? Go to Knitting Class on page 28 and see how it's done.

Monochromatic

Don't forget the opera tickets when you step out wearing this elegant scarf made from shiny ribbon yarn combined with a metallic-blend eyelash yarn. Use the same size needles and the same number of stitches to make this variation, which also requires about the same amount of yarn.

YARN

 Bulky-weight ribbon yarn (A)
*Shown: Crystal Palace Party;
100% nylon; 87 yd (80 m)/1.75
oz (50 g): color #406*

Eyelash yarn (B)
*Shown: Crystal Palace Fizz Stardust;
86% polyester, 14% metallic fiber;
120 yd (110 m)/1.75 oz (50 g): color
#4428*

NEEDLES

Size 13 (9 mm) needles or size
needed to obtain gauge

GAUGE

11 stitches = 4" (10 cm) in seed stitch

Parking and Picking Up

Don't let yourself get confused by the idea of using the eyelash on just some of the rows. It's simpler than you think.

1. Knit two rows with yarn A and yarn B held together.

2. For the next 2 rows, use yarn A by itself. Separate the two yarns if they are twisted, and let go of yarn B. Pick up yarn A and start knitting with it. What to do with yarn B? Just leave it "parked" at the side of the scarf.

3. Complete row 3. Turn and knit another row back (row 4), still using just yarn A.

4. At the beginning of row 5, switch back to using both yarn A and yarn B together again for 2 rows. As you begin this row, notice that yarn B is parked 2 rows below where you are now. Insert your needle to begin a new stitch, wrap yarn A around the stitch but don't pull it through. Pick up yarn B and also wrap it around your needle (it's going to make a little loop along the side of the scarf as it covers the distance from 2 rows below). Now pull both yarn A and yarn B through together and complete the first stitch.

2

4

5. Continue working this row and the next with both yarns held together. Then begin again with step 2.

The only tricky part about this technique is the first stitch of the row when you pick up yarn B again. If you pull too tightly on yarn B as you are adding it back in, you could create a curve in the edge of the scarf. Starting the two yarns separately on the first stitch helps to control the tension.

Beaded Fringe

Here's how to make beaded fringe:

1. Thread the beading needle with about 18" (46 cm) of thread. Anchor the thread at the point where you want to place a bead fringe by knotting the thread and taking one or two small backstitches.

2. String enough beads for the desired length; add one more bead. Skipping the last bead, insert the needle back into the second bead from the end and continue to pass through all of the beads just strung.

3. When you reach the top (the edge of the scarf), take another backstitch into the yarn and continue to the next bead fringe.

4. Repeat steps 1 to 3 across the end of the scarf.

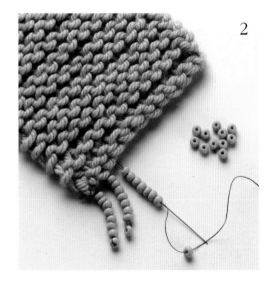

2

Rugged

SUPER BULKY YARN IN EASY RIB STITCH

Novelty yarns usually aren't appropriate for men. There's no way my son would wear a scarf with eyelash. That doesn't mean a guy's scarf can't be luxurious, though. Choose a soft fiber like alpaca, cashmere, or merino and keep the stitch pattern simple. This basic rib-knit scarf, made from a super bulky yarn, knits up so quickly I call it a "one-movie project."

This rib-stitch pattern is known as a one-by-one rib; that is, knit one stitch, purl one stitch across the row. The rib pulls in tightly so it looks as if both sides are knit stitches only, and there isn't a wrong side.

KNIT TIPS

Want to sound like a really good knitter? Ribbing is referred to by the number of knit stitches followed by the number of purl stitches that are used in sequence across a row. So, one-by-one ribbing would be knit one, purl one across the row. Five-by-three rib is knit five, purl three. Get it? As you sip your latte at the next gathering of your knit group, nonchalantly mention that your favorite rib is a three-by-two, and watch the eyebrows rise.

YARN

 Super bulky weight smooth
yarn: 135 yd (123 m)
Shown: Blue Sky Alpacas
Blue Sky Bulky; *50% alpaca, 50% wool;*
45 yd (41 m)/3.5 oz (100 g):
3 hanks color #1010

NEEDLES AND NOTIONS

Size 19 (15 mm) needles or size
needed to obtain gauge

Blunt-end yarn needle

GAUGE

11 stitches = 4" (10 cm) in rib stitch

FINISHED SIZE

4½" × 76" (11.4 × 193 cm)

SCARF

Cast on 12 stitches.

Row 1: * Knit 1, purl 1 *, repeat from * to *
to end of row.

Repeat row 1 until the scarf is the desired
length or until yarn is almost gone, leaving
about 1 yd (0.91 m) to bind off. Bind off
stitches loosely in rib pattern (page 108).

FINISHING

Using the blunt-end yarn needle, weave in all
ends. Don't steam-block this scarf because this
would take away the elasticity of the rib stitch.
The rib of this scarf is meant to pull together.

Tweedy, Finer Texture

Mouline (moo-lean) yarn is made from two or more different colored yarns that are plied together. The tweed look of this masculine scarf is achieved by knitting with a mouline yarn of three different colors. This yarn is much finer than the bulky alpaca so, for a scarf of the same size, you need to use smaller needles and cast on 28 stitches, then follow the same rib pattern. Plan to use about 400 yd (367 m) of yarn if you want to make the scarf 76" (193 cm) long.

YARN

 Medium-weight smooth yarn *Shown: Lana Grossa* Bingo Mouline; *100% merino wool;* 87 yd (80 m)/1.75 oz (50 g): color #804

NEEDLES

Size 9 (5.5 mm) needles or size needed to obtain gauge

GAUGE

24 stitches = 4" (10 cm) in rib stitch

Autumn Chill Chaser

VARIEGATED COLORS IN BROKEN RIB STITCH

There are many different variations of the rib stitch. One way to vary the look is by combining different numbers of knits and purls. Broken rib stitch is another interesting variation. You knit in rib on one side only; on the other side you knit all the way across the row. If you are a little slow in switching between knit and purl stitches, then you'll enjoy this pattern because you can relax and just knit on half of the rows. The scarf shown isn't fringed, but you may choose to add a fringe.

KNIT TIPS

Sometimes it's hard to keep track of what side you are knitting on. If you used the long-tail method to cast on (as taught on pages 106–107), look for the tail that was left over when you finished casting on. If it's on the right side, you are beginning an odd numbered row; if it's on the left side, you are beginning an even numbered row. It's also helpful to mark the odd-numbered row side with a safety pin, moving the pin up as the work progresses.

YARN

 Medium-weight smooth yarn: 280 yd (258 m)
Shown: Alchemy Yarns Lone Star; 55% mohair, 45% merino wool; 140 yd (129 m)/3.5 oz (100 g): 2 hanks color #37c, Early Fall

NEEDLES AND NOTIONS

Size 10 (6 mm) needles or size needed to obtain gauge

Blunt-end yarn needle

GAUGE

16 stitches = 4" (10 cm) in broken rib stitch

FINISHED SIZE

6½" × 70" (16.5 × 178 cm)

SCARF

Cast on 26 stitches.

Row 1: Knit 2, * purl 2, knit 2 *, repeat from * to * to end of row.

Row 2: Knit each stitch to end of row.

Repeat rows 1 and 2, ending with a row 2, until scarf is desired length or until yarn is almost gone, leaving about 1 yd (0.92 m) to bind off.

Bind off stitches loosely in pattern (page 108).

FINISHING

1. Using the blunt-end yarn needle, weave in all ends.
2. Lightly steam block (page 111), gently spreading out the rib as you block the scarf. Though blocking is usually not recommended for ribbed knitting, the broken rib pattern is intended to open up a bit between ribs.

Thick and Thin Yarn

Broken rib stitch pattern looks just as interesting with a thick-and-thin yarn as it does with the smooth yarn. Since this version is made from such a bulky yarn, blocking isn't necessary. Kids just love this funky, chunky look, so keep it away from any teenager in your life or it won't be yours for long. With larger needles, cast on 14 stitches and use 108 yards (99 m) for a waist-length scarf. If you want a longer, thinner scarf using the same amount of yarn, then cast on 10 stitches.

YARN

 Super bulky weight thick-and-thin yarn
Shown: Colinette Point 5; 100% wool; 54 yd (50 m)/3.5 oz (100 g): color #153, Madras

NEEDLES

Size 17 (12.75 mm) needles or size needed to obtain gauge

GAUGE

9 stitches = 4" (10 cm) in broken rib stitch

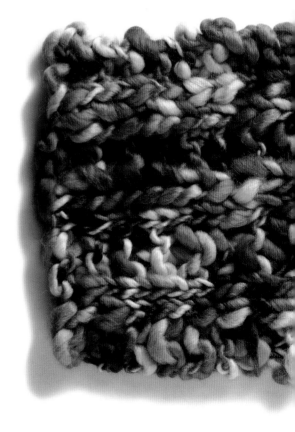

Confetti

MULTI-FIBER YARN IN LACE RIB STITCH

The lace rib stitch pattern creates a lightweight
texture that allows you to knit a summer scarf
using a yarn that might otherwise be too
heavy. The interesting fringe is made by
separating some of the fibers
from the scarf yarn and
combining them with
ribbon yarn.

KNIT TIPS

How do you know when to stop knitting so you will have
enough yarn left over for fringe? Cut your fringe before you
start knitting and set it aside. That way you can knit until you
have just enough yarn left for binding off.

YARN

 Medium-weight multi-fiber yarn: 200 yd (183 m)
Shown: S. Charles Collezione Posh; *50% rayon, 40% polyester, 10% nylon; 81 yd (74 m)/1.75 oz (50 g): 3 balls color #6*

 Medium-weight ribbon yarn, ¼" (6 mm) wide for fringe only: 20 yd (18.3 m)
Shown: Di.Ve' Daitona; 100% nylon; 66 yd (61 m)/0.875 oz (25 g): 1 ball color #00006

NEEDLES AND NOTIONS

Size 10 (6 mm) needles or size needed to obtain gauge

Blunt-end yarn needle

Size 10/J (6 mm) crochet hook

GAUGE

17 stitches = 4" (10 cm) in lace rib stitch

FINISHED SIZE

5½" × 58" (14 × 147 cm), not including fringe

SCARF

Cast on 24 stitches.

Row 1: Knit each stitch to end of row.

Row 2: Knit 2, * yarn over, knit 2 stitches together *, repeat from * to * until 2 stitches remain, knit 2.

Row 3: Knit 1, purl 1, * yarn over, purl 2 stitches together *, repeat from * to * until 2 stitches remain, purl 1, knit 1.

Repeat rows 2 and 3 until scarf is about 58" (147 cm) long.

Last row: Knit each stitch to end of row. Bind off loosely.

FINISHING

Using the blunt-end yarn needle, weave in all ends. Finish by wet blocking (page 111). Making the fringe for this scarf is a little tricky, but well worth the effort. Go to Knitting Class on page 42 to learn the technique.

Warm but Light

This lace rib scarf was knit with one strand of wool and one strand of kid mohair held together, a combination that is warm and soft yet still very lightweight. Using larger needles and 22 stitches, follow the same pattern. Bind off when your scarf is about 64" (163 cm) long. Use the mohair by itself to make fringe: six pieces of mohair in each fringe section, each cut 14" (35.5 cm) long. You will need about 200 yd (183 m) of the wool blend and 250 yd (229 m) of the mohair.

YARN

 Lightweight smooth yarn (A)
Shown: Queensland Collection Kathmandu DK; *85% merino wool, 10% silk, 5% cashmere; 147 yd (135 m)/1.75 oz (50 g): color #417*

Medium-weight kid mohair yarn (B)
Shown: Queensland Collection Comfort Mohair; *80% kid mohair, 15% nylon, 5% wool; 95 yd (87 m)/0.875 oz (25 g): color #417*

NEEDLES

Size 10½ (6.5 mm) needles or size needed to obtain gauge

GAUGE

13 stitches = 4" (10 cm) in lace rib stitch

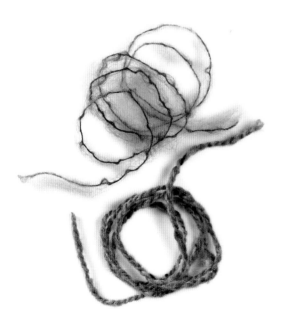

Customized Fringe

I wasn't pleased with how the scarf yarn on page 40 looked when used alone for the fringe. The rayon fiber frayed at the ends and the yarn looked limp. I noticed that the yarn is composed of three different fibers: a shiny rayon core that is variegated from red to yellow, a thin black-and-white braid with confetti flags, and two strands of tiny, almost thread-like bouclé. When I pulled apart the yarn into its components, I realized that the black-and-white braid and the bouclé were very interesting but not meaty enough to be used alone for fringe. The problem was solved by adding ¼" (6 mm) ribbon yarn with a color palette almost identical to the multi-fiber yarn. Here's how to make the fringe:

3

1. Cut 44 pieces of the scarf yarn A, each 14" (35.5 cm) long. Separate the black-and-white braid, bouclé, and rayon fibers of each strand, and discard the rayon fibers. It's actually very easy to separate the fibers for the fringe when you work with these short pieces: Fold the piece in half. At the fold, pinch the shiny rayon strand with one hand. With the other hand, firmly hold the other strands together. Now, gently pull in opposite directions.

2. Cut 44 pieces of the ribbon, each 14" (35.5 cm) long.

3. Arrange 22 fringe bundles, each with two pieces of ribbon yarn, two pieces of black-and-white braid, and four pieces of bouclé.

4. Using the crochet hook, attach one fringe in each space made by the yarnovers at the ends of the scarf; add a fringe close to each side in order to even out the spacing.

5. If desired, trim the fringe to an even length using scissors or a rotary cutter.

4

1

Long and Skinny

STRIPES OF RIBBON AND FUR

I love to knit scarves with stripes. I don't mean "Go Team!" stripes, but stripes that contrast different textures, such as ribbon yarn alternating with shiny fur. This scarf is long and narrow so you can wear it full-length like a rock star or wrap it around your neck a few times and wear it to the PTA meeting.

The two-row stripes run crosswise in the scarf, and the yarn is carried up the side between stripes to avoid having numerous loose ends to weave in. If you've never knit stripes this way, go to Knitting Class on page 48 and practice this technique first with less expensive yarn.

KNIT TIPS

Every time you start a project, make it step one to cut a piece of yarn and tape it to the yarn manufacturer's label. Stash it in a safe place so you can take it with you if you need to buy more of the same yarn. Believe me, your local yarn shop will thank you. Labels tell you laundering instructions, too, and the yarn bit will help you match the scarf to the right label.

YARN

 Bulky-weight fur yarn (A):
60 yd (55 m)
*Shown: Great Adirondack Yarn
Pouf; 100% rayon; 100 yd (92 m)/2.6 oz
(74 g): 1 hank color Mango*

 Super bulky weight ribbon,
½" (13 mm) wide (B): 80 yd
(73 m)
*Shown: Great Adirondack Yarn ½"
Rayon Ribbon; 100% rayon; 100 yd
(92 m)/3.1 oz (88 g): 1 hank color
Mango*

NEEDLES AND NOTIONS

Size 15 (10 mm) needles or size
needed to obtain gauge

Blunt-end yarn needle

Crochet hook, any size

14 large-hole beads for fringe

GAUGE

11 stitches = 4" (10 cm) in garter stitch

FINISHED SIZE

3¾" × 66" (9.5 × 168 cm), not
including fringe

SCARF

Using yarn A, cast on 10 stitches.

Rows 1 and 2: Using yarn A, knit each stitch to
end of row.

Rows 3 and 4: Using yarn B, knit each stitch to
end of row.

Repeat rows 1 to 4 until scarf is desired length.

Using yarn A, knit 2 rows. Bind off loosely.

FINISHING

Using the blunt-end yarn needle, weave in all
ends. You don't need to block this scarf.

FRINGE

The fringe is made from only yarn B, the ribbon.
1. Cut 14 pieces of ribbon, each 24" (61 cm)
   long.
2. Evenly space marks for 7 fringes along each
   short edge. Using a crochet hook, pull one
   end of a ribbon from the back to the front
   through the end of the scarf; make the ends
   even.
3. Cut the ribbon ends at an angle. Working
   with one ribbon at a time, wet the end and
   twist it into a tight point; then push the point
   through the hole in a bead.
4. Even up the ends and slide the bead up to
   the edge of the scarf with one hand while
   holding the ribbon ends with the other hand.
5. Repeat steps 2 to 4, spacing seven fringes
   evenly across each end of the scarf.
6. Cut a clean angled edge on all the ribbon
   ends.

Vanishing Stripes

Yes, this is a striped scarf! Doesn't it look like bright jewels scattered over black velvet? The yarns, a ladder and a bouclé, are both variegated in the same color scheme. Even though you may not be able to see much differ-ence in the stripes, the scarf has a depth and complexity you could not get with one yarn. The yardage requirements are the same but use size 11 (8 mm) needles instead.

YARN

 Medium-weight ladder yarn (A)
Shown: South West Trading Company Calypso; *70% rayon, 20% acrylic, 10% polyester; 109 yd (100 m)/1.75 oz (50 g): color #20*

 Medium-weight multi-fiber bouclé yarn (B)
Shown: S. Charles Collezione Rialto; *57% polyester, 35% rayon, 6% acrylic, 2% nylon; 65 yd (60 m)/1.75 oz (50 g); color Serendipity*

NEEDLES

Size 11 (8 mm) needles or size needed to obtain gauge

GAUGE

11 stitches = 4" (10 cm) in garter stitch

Striping

Sometimes the concept of making stripes with different yarns confuses new knitters. Usually they get into trouble because they're just thinking too much. Here's the inside story about striping.

Choose a smooth medium-weight yarn in two contrasting colors. Using size 10 (6 mm) needles, knit several inches following the pattern below, and keeping the tension loose when you switch from one yarn to the other so the side of the scarf where the yarn is carried doesn't curve.

1. Knit 2 rows with yarn A.

2. On the next row, start using yarn B. What to do with yarn A? Just leave it hanging at the side of the scarf and ignore it for now. Insert your right needle into the first stitch just like you would for any knit stitch (this is the beginning of row 3). Fold yarn B about 6" (15 cm) from the end and loop the fold over the right needle on the back of your knitting. Holding both ends of yarn B, bring the loop through to the front of the stitch on the left needle. You've made a new knit stitch on your right needle.

3. Slide the worked stitch from the left needle off (just like any other knit stitch). Drop the short end of yarn B, and continue across the row using yarn B.

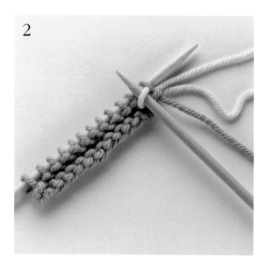

2

4. At the end of row 3, turn and knit another row using yarn B, thus completing row 4.

5. At the beginning of row 5, switch back to yarn A, which you will find hanging 2 rows below where you are now. As before, just stop using the yarn that you used to knit the last 2 rows (yarn B) and leave it hanging on the side of your scarf. Insert your needle to begin a new row, pick up yarn A, and wrap it around your needle just as you would for any knit stitch. Yarn A makes a little, unnoticeable loop along the side of your scarf where it is carried from one stripe up to the next. Don't pull the carried yarn too tightly on the first stitch of the new row; otherwise your scarf will be tighter on one side and have a curved edge.

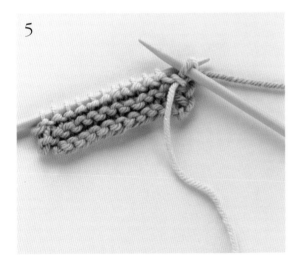

6. Continue in this manner, knitting 2 rows with yarn A and 2 rows with yarn B, until you reach the desired length.

A New Direction

SELF-STRIPING YARN KNITTED LENGTHWISE

My customers are often surprised when they discover they can knit a scarf sideways. Sideways? Sure. Instead of casting on a few stitches and knitting a lot of rows until the scarf is long enough, you cast on a lot of stitches (equal to the length of the scarf) and knit a few rows until the scarf is wide enough. Straight needles are too short to hold this many stitches, so use a circular needle with a long cable instead. This is a very effective technique to use with self-striping yarn because the resulting scarf will have vertical stripes instead of horizontal stripes. Caution: knitting with self-striping yarns can be addictive—you can't wait to see what the next color is going to be. You may find yourself staying up too late to knit just one more row.

KNIT TIPS

The biggest challenge to knitting scarves sideways, or lengthwise, is making the cast-on and bind-off edges loose enough. If one edge is too tight, the scarf will curve toward the tight side. If both edges are too tight, the middle can pucker. The solution is to use a larger needle for casting on and binding off. Use the smaller needle for all the other rows.

YARN

Super bulky self-striping yarn: 120 yd (108 m)

Shown: Nashua Handknits
Equinox Stripe; *73% wool, 27% acrylic; 66 yd (61 m)/3.5 oz (100 g): 2 balls color EQS 108, Smoothie*

NEEDLES AND NOTIONS

Size 19 (15 mm) circular needle or size needed to obtain gauge, at least 24" (61 cm) long

Size 17 (12.75 mm) circular needle or size needed to obtain gauge, at least 24" (61 cm) long

Blunt-end yarn needle

GAUGE

7.5 stitches = 4" (10 cm) in garter stitch

FINISHED SIZE

4" × 68" (10 × 173 cm), not including fringe

SCARF

Measure about 7 or 8 yards (6.4 or 7.3 m) of yarn and make your slipknot (that's a really long tail). Using the larger needle, cast on 125 stitches.

Row 1: Switch to the smaller needle. Knit each stitch to end of row.

Repeat row 1 until the scarf reaches the desired width, saving at least 10 to 11 yd (9 to 10 m) for binding off.

Switch to the larger needle and bind off loosely.

FINISHING

Using the blunt-end yarn needle, weave in all ends. If desired, steam very lightly to block (page 111).

FRINGE

1. Cut 16 pieces of yarn, each 15" (38 cm) long. If desired, match the fringe colors to the stripe colors in the scarf.
2. Evenly space eight fringes along each short edge. Pull one end of the fringe through the scarf and even up the ends. Then tie both ends together in an overhand knot close to the scarf edge.
3. Trim the ends even, if you like.

Subtle Suede

Once you learn to knit scarves sideways, you'll want to try it with many different yarns. For the body of the scarf, choose a needle that's the same size or slightly bigger than the recommendation on the yarn's label. For casting on and binding off, use a needle that is one or two sizes larger than the needle used for the body of the scarf. As you can see from this variation, sideways knitting works beautifully with solid color yarn, too. This suede yarn, with its subtle color shading, makes a very unusual, touchable texture.

To make this variation, cast on 280 stitches with a size 9 (5.5 mm) circular needle. You'll need about 250 yards (228 m). Use a needle one size smaller to knit the scarf but switch back to the larger needle for binding off.

YARN

Medium-weight suede ribbon yarn

Shown: Berroco Suede; *100% nylon; 120 yd (110 m)/1.75 oz (50 g): color #3751*

NEEDLES

Size 9 (5.5 mm) circular needle or size needed to obtain gauge, at least 24" (61 cm) long

Size 8 (5 mm) circular needle or size needed to obtain gauge, at least 24" (61 cm) long

GAUGE

17 stitches = 4" (10 cm) in garter stitch

Quick Twist

RIBBON YARN IN TWISTED DROP STITCH

This unusual scarf is knit sideways using a clever stitch that's twisted and greatly elongated compared to a normal knit stitch. It sounds complicated, but it's very easy and insanely fast. If you need to make a few scarves in an evening, you can do it with this design. December 23 should no longer make you break out into a cold sweat. This stitch can also be easy on the budget since a scarf uses only about 75 yards (69 meters) of yarn. Go to Knitting Class on page 58, if you've never knitted twisted drop stitches.

KNIT TIPS

Read all the directions for a pattern before you start knitting. At least you'll be sure you have all the supplies you need. Can you imagine anything worse than settling in for a cozy night of knitting and finding out that you're missing a ball of yarn or a special needle?

YARN

 Super bulky ribbon yarn:
75 yd (69 m)
Shown: Filati FF Jolliet Multi;
*88% nylon, 12% polyester; 47 yd
(43 m)/1.75 oz (50 g): 2 balls color
#206*

NEEDLES AND NOTIONS

Size 17 (12.75 mm) circular needle or
size needed to obtain gauge, at least
24" (61 cm) long

Size 15 (10 mm) circular needle or
size needed to obtain gauge, at least
24" (61 cm) long

Blunt-end yarn needle

GAUGE

7½ stitches = 4" (10 cm) in twisted
drop stitch

FINISHED SIZE

3¼" × 60" (8.2 × 152.5 cm)

SCARF

Using the larger needle, cast on 110 stitches
(you will need at least 5 yd [4.6 m] of yarn for
the tail).

Row 1: Switch to the smaller needle. Knit each
stitch to end of row.

Row 2: Knit each stitch to end of row.

Row 3: Knit all stitches in twisted drop stitch.

Row 4: Knit each stitch to end of row.

Row 5: Knit each stitch to end of row.

Row 6: Knit all stitches in twisted drop stitch.

Row 7: Knit each stitch to end of row.

Row 8: Knit each stitch to end of row.

Switch to the larger needle and bind off very
loosely.

FINISHING

Using the blunt-end yarn needle, weave in all
ends. Do not block.

Tighter Twist

Twisted drop stitch is one of those patterns that is fun to try with many different yarns. The basic pattern can be repeated until the scarf is wide enough. Choose a needle that is a few sizes larger than recommended on the yarn label; the needle for casting on and binding off should be even larger. The gently modulated colors of this kettle-dyed, thick-and-thin wool from Uruguay look very pretty, especially with a bit of ribbon for a fringe. The result is super lightweight, warm, and wonderful. For an average length scarf, you'll need about 125 yards (114 m). Cast on 135 stitches using a size 10½ (6.5 mm) needle. Follow the basic pattern using a size 10 (6 mm) needle, adding two more pattern repeats (knit two rows, twisted drop stitch one row).

YARN

Medium-weight thick-and-thin yarn
Shown: Manos del Uruguay Yarn Kettle-Dyed Wool; 100% wool; 138 yd (127 m)/3.5 oz (100 g); color #68

NEEDLES

Size 10½ (6.5 mm) circular needle or size needed to obtain gauge, at least 24" (61 cm) long

Size 10 (6 mm) circular needle or size needed to obtain gauge, at least 4" (61 cm) long

GAUGE

9 stitches = 4" (10 cm) in twisted drop stitch

Twisted Drop Stitch

Twisted drop stitch is easy to learn, so grab some scrap yarn from your stash and give it a try.

1. Cast on 10 stitches and knit a row (the entire pattern is worked in knit stitch—no purling).

2. On the second row, for the twisted drop stitch, insert the needle into the first stitch. Wrap the yarn around both needles and then around the right (back) needle like a regular knit stitch.

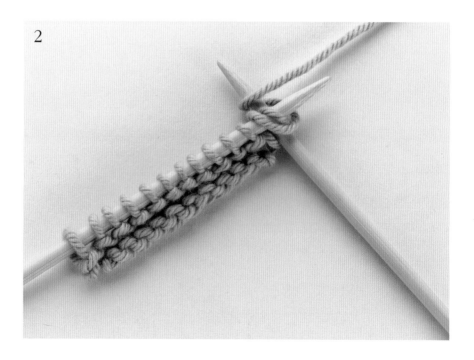

2

3. Now complete the knit stitch as always by pulling the loop on the right needle through. Note that you have two loops around your left needle; just treat them as a single strand (that second loop is what will become the elongated part of the stitch), and slide them off the needle.

4. Complete the row, following steps 2 and 3 with every stitch.

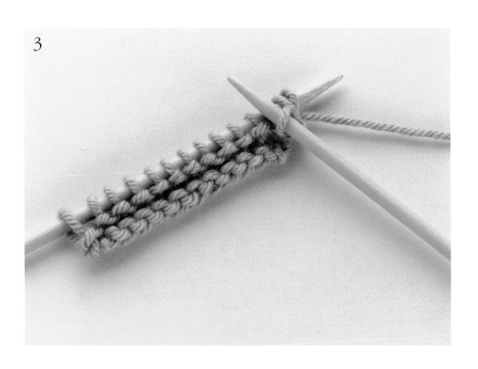

Decadence

MULTIPLE YARNS IN TWISTED DROP STITCH

There are so many beautiful yarns in my shop, sometimes it's hard for me to control myself. Even I want to buy one of everything and I own the place! The idea for this shawl came to me when I was looking for yarns to make a red-and-gold scarf. So many yarns looked wonderful together, it was hard to choose—so I decided to use all of them. Twisted drop stitch (page 58) was an obvious choice for the pattern because it uses less yarn and is relatively lightweight. Believe it or not, this project is knit with all four yarns held together at the same time. The stitches are so bulky that you'll finish in no time, but rushing might cause problems. Just slow down and let yourself get wrapped up in the beauty of these yarns.

KNIT TIPS

Many of the yarns we knit with are imported from Europe and Asia, where the metric system is used. Usually a yarn label will be marked with both measurements, but if you have to convert from metric, here's all you need to know.

1 inch = 2.54 centimeters
1 yard = 0.9144 meters
1 meter = 1.094 yards
1 ounce = 28.35 grams
1 gram = 0.0353 ounces

YARN

 Bulky-weight ribbon yarn (A): 150 yd (137 m)
Shown: Katia Chic; 54% wool, 43% nylon, 3% polyester; 70 yd (64 m)/1.75 oz (50 g): 3 balls color #20

 Medium-weight smooth yarn (B): 150 yd (137 m)
Shown: Plymouth/Filati Bertagna Palma; 60% wool, 38% nylon, 2% Lurex; 110 yd (101 m)/1.75 oz (50 g): 2 balls color #800

 Medium-weight novelty bouclé yarn (C): 150 yd (137 m)
Shown: Plymouth Meteor; 90% nylon, 10% Lurex; 234 yd (215 m)/1.75 oz (50 g): 1 ball color #1518

Novelty eyelash yarn (D): 150 yd (137 m)
Shown: Habu Textiles Poly Moire; 100% polyester; 23 yd (21 m)/0.5 oz (14 g): 7 balls color #11

NEEDLES AND NOTIONS

Size 19 (15 mm) circular needle or size needed to obtain gauge, at least 24" (61 cm) long
Blunt-end yarn needle

GAUGE

6 stitches = 4" (10 cm) in twisted drop stitch

FINISHED SIZE

14" × 45" (35.5 × 115 cm)

SHAWL

With all four yarns held together, cast on 22 stitches.

Row 1: Knit all stitches in twisted drop stitch.

Row 2: Knit each stitch to end of row.

Repeat rows 1 and 2 until the shawl is the desired length (about 30 times), saving at least 3 yd (2.74 m) for binding off.

Bind off very loosely.

FINISHING

Using the blunt-end yarn needle, weave in all ends. Do not block.

Black and White

Black and white together can be a showstopper! This scarf is like a snow-storm on Fifth Avenue—fun yet sophisticated. This particular foursome of yarns creates a looser, lighter weight fabric than the red shawl. To get the same size shawl, you only need to cast on 18 stitches and buy about 125 yd (114 m) of each yarn.

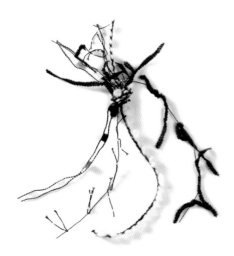

YARN

 Medium-weight bouclé yarn (A) *Shown: Katia* Cocktail; *40% wool, 40% acrylic, 20% poly-ester; 82 yd (75 m)/1.75 oz (50 g): color #3*

 Medium-weight ladder yarn (B) *Shown: Plymouth* Eros; *100% nylon; 165 yd (152 m)/1.75 oz (50 g): color #1024*

Novelty eyelash yarn (C) *Shown: Habu Textiles* Kasumi; *100% polyester; 60 yd (55 m)/0.5 oz (14 g): color #10*

Chenille eyelash yarn (D) *Shown: Habu Textiles* Feather Moire; *83% polyester, 17% nylon; 23 yd (21 m)/0.5 oz (14 g): color #10*

NEEDLES

Size 19 (15 mm) circular needle or size needed to obtain gauge, at least 24" (61 cm) long

GAUGE

5 stitches = 4" (10 cm) in twisted drop stitch

The Ruffle Effect

KNITTED SIDEWAYS WITH ACCENT EDGING

What's more feminine than ruffles? This scarf is one continuous ruffle knitted sideways on a circular needle. Every other row, you double the number of stitches by knitting twice into each stitch. Check the basics on page 110 to see how it's done. The multi-fiber, multicolor yarn gives the scarf remarkable texture and depth. A contrast yarn, used only for the bind-off row, defines the edge and adds a subtle bit of sparkle.

KNIT TIPS

Be nice to your scarf—don't hang it. How would you like to sleep standing up? Hanging may cause a scarf to stretch, especially if it has been knit loosely. Instead, fold it and lay it flat for storage.

YARN

 Medium-weight multi-fiber yarn (A): 150 yd (137 m)
Shown: Fiesta Yarns La Boheme (2-strand yarn); first strand 64% brushed kid mohair, 28% wool, 8% nylon; second strand 100% rayon bouclé; 165 yd (152 m)/4 oz (113 g): 1 hank color #11104, Caribbean

 Medium-weight novelty yarn (B): 50 yd (46 m)
Shown: Crystal Palace Little Flowers; 66% rayon, 30% nylon, 4% metallic fiber; 145 yd (133 m)/1.75 oz (50 g): 1 ball color #9757

NEEDLES AND NOTIONS

Size 15 (10 mm) circular needle or size needed to obtain gauge, at least 24" (61 cm) long

Blunt-end yarn needle

GAUGE

6½ stitches = 4" (10 cm) along the cast-on (unruffled) edge

FINISHED SIZE

2¼" × 60" (5.7 × 152.4 cm)

SCARF

Using yarn A, cast on 96 stitches.

Row 1: Knit each stitch to end of row.

Row 2: Knit into the front and back of every stitch—at the end of this row, you should have 192 stitches.

Row 3: Knit each stitch to end of row.

Row 4: Knit into the front and back of every stitch—at the end of this row, you should have 384 stitches.

Row 5: Knit each stitch to end of row.

Row 6: Knit into the front and back of every stitch—at the end of this row, you should have 768 stitches.

Row 7: Knit each stitch to end of row.

Change to yarn B and bind off.

FINISHING

Using the blunt-end yarn needle, weave in all ends. Do not block.

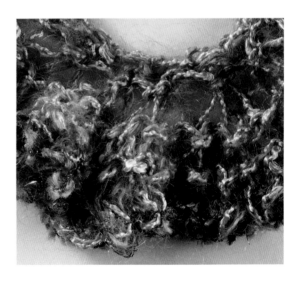

Soft and Fuzzy

To create this soft and fuzzy ruffle scarf, a fur yarn and mohair yarn are knit together—the fur for luxurious softness and the mohair for extra body. A metallic cord yarn, used only for binding off, edges the ruffle with a touch of color and sparkle. Since this yarn combination is somewhat heavier, use a larger needle and cast on just 85 to 90 stitches. Use two strands of the metallic cord (yarn C) held together for the bind off. You will need about 150 yards (137 m) of both yarn A and yarn B and 50 yards (46 m) of yarn C.

YARN

Super bulky weight fur yarn (A)
Shown: Muench Yarns/GGH Amelie; 100% microfiber nylon; 71 yd (65 m)/1.75 oz (50 g): color #03

Medium-weight mohair yarn (B)
Shown: Katia Igenua; 78% mohair, 13% nylon, 9% wool; 153 yd (141 m)/1.75 oz (50 g): color #21

Lightweight smooth yarn (C)
Shown: Ironstone Yarns Paris Nights; 67% acrylic, 21% nylon, 12% metal; 202 yd (185 m)/1.75 oz (50 g): color #30

NEEDLES

Size 17 (12.75 mm) circular needle or size needed to obtain gauge, at least 24" (61 cm) long

GAUGE

$6\frac{1}{4}$ stitches = 4" (10 cm) along the cast-on (unruffled) edge

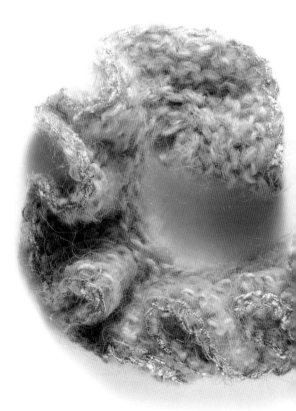

Happy Endings

CONTRASTING RUFFLES ON THE ENDS

Scarves often benefit from an interesting finish on the ends; usually it's a fringe, but a knitted ruffle is also beautiful and dramatic. Made in a contrasting yarn, the ruffle is easy to make and utterly feminine. This scarf combines two yarns: the body is made from silk and the ruffle is made from bamboo. Yes bamboo! The feeling against your neck is unimaginably luxurious.

This scarf begins as a very basic seed stitch scarf that is bound off and blocked before the ruffle is added. The ruffle is made by picking up stitches along the short edges after the scarf is finished. You can review how to pick up stitches on pages 110–111.

KNIT TIPS

Mistakes are much easier to fix if you discover them quickly. As you are knitting, pause frequently to examine your work. Pull it down gently away from the needle. Are any stitches dropped or incomplete? Count your stitches; do you have the same number as when you started?

YARN

 Lightweight smooth yarn (A): 110 yd (101 m)
Shown: Fiesta Yarns La Luz; 100% silk; 220 yd (202 m)/2 oz (57 g): 1 hank color #3321, Aleutian Green

 Lightweight smooth yarn (B): 70 yd (64 m)
Shown: Alchemy Yarns Bamboo; 100% bamboo; 150 yd (138 m)/1.75 oz (50 g): 1 hank color #43, Waterlily

NEEDLES AND NOTIONS

Size 6 (4 mm) needles or size needed to obtain gauge

Blunt-end yarn needle

GAUGE

21 stitches = 4" (10 cm) in seed stitch

FINISHED SIZE

4" × 38" (10 × 97 cm) including ruffle

SCARF

Using yarn A, cast on 21 stitches.

Row 1: * Knit 1, purl 1 *, repeat from * to * until 1 stitch remains, end with knit 1.

Repeat row 1 until scarf is about 34" (86.5 cm) long. Bind off loosely.

Wet block (page 111) the scarf before adding the ruffle.

RUFFLE

Working from the right side, using yarn B, pick up and knit 21 stitches.

Row 1: Knit each stitch to end of row.

Row 2: * Knit 1, yarn over *, repeat from * to * until 1 stitch remains, end with knit 1. You should have 41 stitches.

Rows 3 to 5: Knit each stitch to end of row.

Row 6: * Knit 1, yarn over *, repeat from * to * until 1 stitch remains, end with knit 1. You should have 81 stitches.

Rows 7 to 9: Knit each stitch to end of row.

Row 10: Knit 1 * yarn over, knit 2 together *, repeat from * to * to end of row.
Note that row 10 doesn't increase the number of stitches. The yarnovers are simply used to create decorative eyelet holes.

Rows 11 to 13: Knit each stitch to end of row.

Bind off loosely.

Repeat ruffle for other end of scarf.

FINISHING

Using the blunt-end yarn needle, weave in all ends. Don't block after the ruffle is attached; you don't want to flatten it.

Bumpy Endings

A ruffled finish can also turn a warm winter scarf into a fashion statement. Since you want the scarf to drape nicely, knit the ruffle with a light-weight yarn that won't drag it down. For this light-as-a-feather alpaca blend scarf, I used the same size needle and the same number of stitches. You'll need about 110 yards (101 m) for the main scarf and 70 yards (64 m) for the ruffle.

YARN

 Lightweight smooth wool yarn (A)
Shown: Classic Elite Yarns Miracle; 50% alpaca, 50% tencel; 108 yd (99 m)/1.75 oz (50 g): color #3395

 Fine-weight bouclé yarn (B)
Shown: Wool in the Woods Wilkson; 93% wool, 7% nylon; 200 yd (184 m)/1.75 oz (50 g): color Lottery

NEEDLES

Size 6 (4 mm) needles or size needed to obtain gauge

GAUGE

17 stitches = 4" (10 cm) in seed stitch

Gossamer Odyssey

FUNKY BOUCLÉ ON A WEB OF MOHAIR

The success of this design depends on choosing two yarns of extremely different textures and weights. The heavy yarn should be a bouclé or thick-and-thin yarn—the crazier, the better. The mohair should be very lightweight and smooth. The much heavier bouclé careens wildly across the spider web background of the delicate mohair. For even more interest, the scarf ends are flared. Knitting this scarf on a circular needle accommodates the width and allows you to make stripes consisting of an odd number of rows. Intrigued? Discover the secrets in Knitting Class on page 76.

KNIT TIPS

Don't we all knit on the run—at the airport, in the doctor's office, waiting to pick up a kid? It never fails: when you need to measure something, you don't have a ruler. Did you know that U.S. currency is 6" (15 cm) long? An average woman's hand spread wide is 8" (20.5 cm); the middle bone of your little finger is about 1" (2.5 cm) long; and a standard sheet of paper is 8½" x 11" (22 x 28 cm). If you're going to knit on the road, it helps to be resourceful.

YARN

 Bulky-weight bouclé yarn (A): 90 yd (82 m)
Shown: S. Charles Collezione Sabrina; 45% wool, 24% cotton, 16% rayon, 9% acrylic, 6% nylon; 60 yd (55 m)/1.75 oz (50 g): 2 balls color #23

 Lightweight mohair yarn (B): 134 yd (123 m)
Shown: Crystal Palace Kid Merino; 28% kid merino, 28% merino, 44% micronylon; 240 yd (221 m)/0.875 oz (25 g): 1 ball color #4673, Espresso

NEEDLES AND NOTIONS

Size 13 (9 mm) circular needle or size needed to obtain gauge, at least 16" (41 cm) long

Blunt-end yarn needle

GAUGE

15 stitches = 4" (10 cm) in garter stitch

FINISHED SIZE

5½" × 53" (14 × 134.5 cm)

SCARF

Beginning with one flared end, using yarn A, cast on 60 stitches.

Rows 1 to 3: Change to yarn B. Knit each stitch using yarn B. NOTE: Be sure to use yarn B, the mohair, to catch yarn A, the bouclé, along the edge of the scarf when you begin a new row from a side where yarn A has been parked (see page 77). Do this between every second and third row of mohair.

Row 4: Knit each stitch using yarn A.

Rows 5 and 6: Knit each stitch using yarn B.

Row 7: Using yarn B, * knit 2 together *, repeat from * to * across row—30 stitches remain.

Row 8: Knit each stitch using yarn A.
Rows 9 to 11: Knit each stitch using yarn B.

Row 12: Knit each stitch using yarn A.

Rows 13 and 14: Knit each stitch using yarn B.

Row 15: Using yarn B, * knit 1, knit 2 together *, repeat from * to * across row—20 stitches remain.

Row 16: Knit each stitch using yarn A.

Begin narrow body of the scarf.

Rows 1 and 2: Knit each stitch using yarn B.

Row 3: Knit each stitch using yarn A. Continue repeating rows 1 to 3 until the scarf is about 47" (120 cm) long.

Begin flared end.

Row 1: Knit each stitch using yarn B.

Row 2: Using yarn B, * knit 1, increase 1 *, repeat from * to * across row (knit into the front and back of every stitch)—you will have 30 stitches.

Row 3: Knit each stitch using yarn B.

Row 4: Knit each stitch using yarn A.

Rows 5 to 7: Knit each stitch using yarn B.

Row 8: Knit each stitch using yarn A.

Row 9: Knit each stitch using yarn B.

Row 10: Using yarn B, * increase 1 *, repeat from * to * across row—you will have 60 stitches.

Row 11: Knit each stitch using yarn B.

Row 12: Knit each stitch using yarn A.

Rows 13 to 15: Knit each stitch using yarn B.

Bind off loosely using yarn A.

FINISHING

Using the blunt-end yarn needle, weave in all ends. Do not block.

A Little Tamer

This thick-and-thin yarn is, shall we say, more demure than that in the first version. The result is still pretty wild, but the more subdued color allows the structure to be seen more clearly. The effect is further enhanced by the subtle color changes in the thick-and-thin yarn.

Use the same size needle and the same number of stitches. This scarf will be slightly wider than the first version. If you want the main body of the scarf to be narrower, start with 54 stitches; even narrower, start with 48 stitches. Yardage requirements are about the same.

YARN

 Bulky-weight thick-and-thin yarn (A)
Shown: Moda Dea Caché; 75% wool, 22% acrylic, 3% polyester; 72 yd (66 m)/1.75 oz (50 g): color #2355

4 Medium-weight mohair (B)
Shown: Madil Yarns Kid Seta; 70% super kid mohair, 30% silk; 229 yd (211 m)/0.875 oz (25 g): color #830

NEEDLES

Size 13 (9 mm) circular needle or size needed to obtain gauge, at least 16" (40.5 cm) long

GAUGE

12 stitches = 4" (10 cm) in garter stitch

Stripes with Odd Numbers of Rows

When you make stripes with even numbered rows, the yarn you "parked" two rows before is waiting for you along the right edge when you are ready to pick it up again. But what happens when you want to make a stripe with an odd number of rows or just a single row? The parked yarn ends up on the left side, a problem easily solved with a circular needle. Grab two contrasting yarns and a circular needle and follow these steps to learn how it's done.

1. Using yarn A, cast on a few stitches and knit three rows, turning the circular needle back and forth as if you were using two straight needles.

2. Switch to yarn B and knit three rows.

3. Now, hold up the needle with the side you just finished facing you, the stitches are on the left and the empty needle is on the right. See yarn A hanging on the right side three rows below? Instead of turning the needle, push the stitches from the left side to the right side of the needle.

3

4. Pick up yarn A (it will make a loop along the side) and start knitting.

As you follow these steps, on every other set of rows, the parked yarn will end up on the same side you just finished, so you turn the needle in the conventional way, rather than slide the stitches to the right. The directions don't tell you whether to turn the needle or push the stitches. Here's how you will know: When you finish a row, hold up your knitting and determine where the working yarn is for the next row. If it's on the left side (1), turn the needle around and begin the next row. If the working yarn is on the right side (2), push the stitches back over to the right side of the needle to begin the next row.

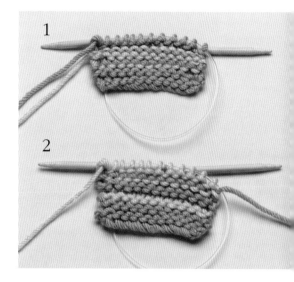

When yarn is parked for more than two rows, you need to take it along for the ride up the side of the scarf. Here's how it's done: After you've finished knitting two rows with yarn A, the strand of yarn B will be hanging two rows below. Before starting the next row, loop yarn A under yarn B, as in the photo at right (actually pick up the entire ball of yarn A and move it under yarn B). Then begin knitting with yarn A again. This "catches" yarn B, making an almost invisible loop around it and moving it up along the side of the scarf.

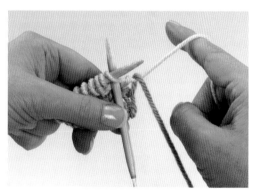

Your Feminine Side

RUFFLES AND LACE

Ruffles, lace, and drama. When you wear this shawl to your next party, be sure to arrive late—you wouldn't want to waste a wrap this gorgeous with a punctual arrival. This shawl will allow you to use several skills on the same project. You'll be knitting sideways on a circular needle, beginning and ending with a ruffle, and the body is an easy lace stitch. It's not as tricky as it sounds, but there is one step that might make you nervous. You need to cast on a lot of stitches for the bottom ruffle—a whole lot of stitches. That's why you need such a long needle; it's the only way to fit all of the beginning stitches. In Knitting Class on page 82, I'll teach you two tricks to make casting on the stitches easier.

KNIT TIPS

When you are knitting with lots of stitches, it's easy to accidentally add a stitch or knit too many stitches together. Don't panic, just fake it. At the end of the row, if you have two stitches and you're only supposed to have one, just knit them together. No one will ever notice.

YARN

Lightweight smooth rayon yarn: 875 yd (800 m)
Shown: Blue Heron Yarns
Rayon Metallic; *88% rayon, 12% metallic; 550 yd (501 m)/7.4 oz (210 g): 2 hanks color Hibiscus*

NEEDLES AND NOTIONS

Size 6 (4 mm) circular needle or size needed to obtain gauge, at least 40" (102 cm) long

Blunt-end yarn needle

GAUGE

19 stitches = 4" (10 cm) in lace stitch

FINISHED SIZE

11" × 72" (28 × 183 cm)

SHAWL

Beginning with deeper ruffle at bottom of shawl, cast on 1,200 stitches (you can do it).

Row 1: Knit each stitch to end of row.

Row 2: Purl each stitch to end of row.

Row 3: Knit each stitch to end of row.

Row 4: Purl 1, * yarn over, purl 2 together *, repeat from * to * to last stitch, purl 1.

Row 5: Knit each stitch to end of row.

Row 6: Purl each stitch to end of row.

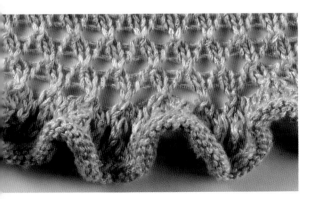

Row 7: * Knit 2 together *, repeat from * to * to end of row—600 stitches (it's getting easier already).

Row 8: Purl 1, * yarn over, purl 2 together *, repeat from * to * to last stitch, purl 1.

Row 9: Knit each stitch to end of row.

Row 10: Purl each stitch to end of row.

Row 11: * Knit 2 together *, repeat from * to * to end of row—300 stitches (piece of cake).

Body of shawl in an all-over lace pattern:

Row 1: Purl 1, * yarn over, purl 2 together *, repeat from * to * to last stitch, purl 1.

Row 2: Knit each stitch to end of row.

Row 3: Purl each stitch to end of row.

Row 4: Knit each stitch to end of row.

Rows 1 to 4 make up the lace pattern for the body of the shawl. Repeat these four rows 20 more times (a total of 84 rows).

Narrower ruffle at top of shawl:

Row 1: Purl 1, * yarn over, purl 2 together *, repeat from * to * to last stitch, purl 1.

Row 2: Knit into the front and back of every stitch, including the yarnovers—600 stitches (getting a little hot in here).

Row 3: Knit into the front and back of every stitch—1,200 stitches (déjà vu all over again).

Row 4: Knit each stitch to end of row.

Row 5: Bind off in knit stitch (even though you will be on a purl side).

FINISHING

Using the blunt-end yarn needle, weave in all ends. Don't block this shawl. Also, be sure to store it flat, not hanging, so it doesn't stretch out of shape.

In Bouclé

You can use this versatile pattern to experiment with a wide variety of yarns—just use a needle that is the same size or slightly larger than the recommendation on the label. To make the shawl shorter (end to end), cast on fewer stitches. Just be sure that you always work with an even number of stitches. The basic pattern is the same. This version is knit with a lustrous rayon yarn that's approximately the same weight but has a rougher texture. Use the same size needle but cast on fewer stitches, since this yarn knits at a slightly heavier gauge. To make the same size shawl, you'll need about 750 yards (683 m). If you want to make a shorter shawl that is about 50" (127 cm) long, cast on 800 stitches.

YARN

 Lightweight bouclé yarn
Shown: Wool in the Woods Cruz;
100% rayon; 200 yd (184 m)/
3.25 oz (92 g): color Bashful

NEEDLES

Size 6 (4mm) circular needle or size needed to obtain gauge, at least 40" (102) long

GAUGE

16 stitches = 4" (10 cm) in lace stitch

Casting On Big Time

You need to cast on 1,200 stitches, so how long should the tail be? Try this:

Wrap the yarn around the needle 12 times. Take the yarn off and measure it. It should be about 8" (20.5 cm) long and that's $\frac{1}{100}$ the length you will need in total (1,200 stitches divided by 12). So, 8" (20.5 cm) × 100 = 800" (2,050 cm) or 66 feet (201 m). Using the Five Foot Rule (page 95), that would mean stretching the yarn from fingertip to fingertip about 13 to 14 times. Throw in a couple extra fingertip stretches. It would be far better to waste a few feet of yarn than to have to start casting on all over again.

1

How in the world do you keep count of 1,200 stitches to cast on? Just get it right 100 stitches at a time.

1. Cut a contrast yarn into 11 pieces, each 4" (10 cm) long, to make stitch markers. Tie each piece into a loop, using an overhand knot.

2. Cast on 100 stitches and double-check to make sure you're correct. Now, put a marker in between these stitches and the next 100 (just slip the stitch marker over the needle). You know all the stitches to the right of the marker are correctly counted. Remember to remove the stitch markers when you knit the first row.

2

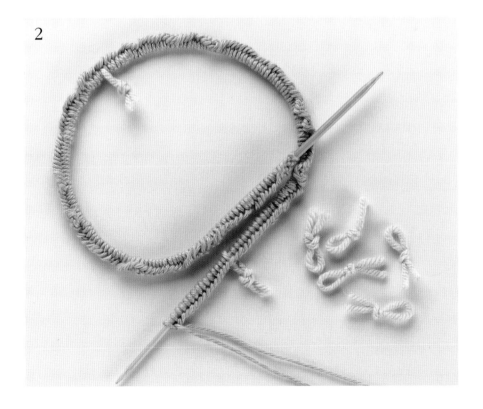

Scrumptious

MEDLEY OF TEXTURES AND COLORS

I made this shawl the first time for my mother-in-law, Luana. It had to be beautiful because she has fabulous taste; it also had to be lightweight, since she lives in California. Generous amounts of mohair kept it lightweight, and the addition of chenille and rayon bouclé added luxurious depth. The finished garment is turned into a showstopper with the addition of the amazing fringe that incorporates the yarns from the shawl and numerous hand-dyed silk ribbons. Luana loved her shawl.

KNIT TIPS

When it's time for me to measure fringe for cutting, I usually grab whatever is sitting on the coffee table (with three kids, there's usually a lot of stuff). A DVD case makes the perfect tool for measuring fringe. Wrap your yarn all the way around the case once for each fringe. I usually wrap the long way for adult scarves and the short way for kids. Slip sharp scissors between the case and the yarn at the beginning of the wrap, and cut.

YARN

 Medium-weight multi-fiber yarn (A): 165 yd (151 m)
Shown: Fiesta Yarns La Boheme (2-strand yarn); first strand 64% brushed kid mohair, 28% wool, 8% nylon; second strand 100% rayon bouclé; 165 yd (152 m)/4 oz (113 g): 1 hank color #11254, Safari

 Bulky-weight bouclé yarn (B): 90 yd (82 m)
Shown: Colinette Zanziba; 51% wool, 48% rayon, 1% nylon; 103 yd (95 m)/3.5 oz (100 g): 1 hank color #135, Sahara

 Super bulky weight rayon chenille yarn (C): 90 yd (83 m)
Shown: Colinette Isis; 100% rayon; 109 yd (100 m)/3.5 oz (100 g): 1 hank color #112, Velvet Gold

Hand-dyed silk ribbon, various colors to coordinate with yarn in widths from ⅝" to 1½" (15 to 39 mm): total of 10 to 12 yd (9.1 to 11 m)
Shown: Artemis Hand Dyed Silk Ribbon

NEEDLES AND NOTIONS

Size 13 (9 mm) circular needle or size needed to obtain gauge, at least 24" (61 cm) long

Size 15 (10 mm) circular needle or size needed to obtain gauge, at least 24" (61 cm) long

Safety pins

Size 10/J (6 mm) or larger crochet hook

Blunt-end yarn needle

GAUGE

8 stitches = 4" (10 cm) in garter stitch

FINISHED SIZE

9" × 72" (23 × 183 cm), not including fringe

SHAWL

Using yarn A and the larger needle, cast on 148 stitches.

Rows 1 to 3: Switch to the smaller needle. Knit every stitch using yarn A.

Rows 4 to 5: Knit every stitch using yarn B.

Rows 6 to 7: Knit every stitch using yarn C.

NOTE: Remember to carry the parked yarns up the sides of the shawl (page 77).

Repeat rows 1 to 7 five more times (total of 42 rows). Each time you change yarns, push the stitches to the right when the parked yarn you want to pick up is on the right. Turn the needle when the parked yarn you want to pick up is on the left.

Knit three rows with yarn A.

Switch to the larger needle and bind off very loosely.

FINISHING

Using the blunt-end yarn needle, weave in all ends. If desired, steam very lightly (page 111).

FRINGE

1. From each of the three yarns, cut 22 pieces, each 15" (38 cm) long. Arrange the pieces into 22 groups with one piece of each yarn per group.
2. Cut the silk ribbons into 22 pieces, each 15" (38 cm) long. Scatter the various widths and colors among the fringe groups.
3. Measure and mark with a safety pin the location for 11 fringes spaced evenly across each end of the scarf.
4. Use the crochet hook to pull through all four strands at once and tie each fringe. If desired, cut the ribbon ends at a slant.

A Different Trio

When I find a technique that works well, I want to try it with every yarn in the shop. I used the same beautiful stripe sequence to combine a completely different grouping of yarn, including some ribbon. You'll notice that the stitch is a little bit finer than the first version. Normally you would need to cast on more stitches in order for the finished length to be the same. However, this is a very stretchy combination, so stick to the same number of stitches and it should be about the same length when worn. To be safe, purchase about 10 percent more yardage than the first version.

YARN

 Bulky-weight multi-fiber arn (A)
Shown: Muench Yarns/GGH Oceana; 55% rayon, 30% nylon, 15% cotton; 77 yd (71 m)/1.75 oz (50 g): color #4802

 Bulky-weight ribbon yarn (B)
Shown: Filatura di Crosa Malva; 85% cotton, 15% nylon; 109 yd (100 m)/1.75 oz (50 g): color #2

 Bulky-weight bouclé yarn (C)
Shown: Berroco Monet; 42% rayon, 36% acrylic, 13% cotton, 9% nylon; 49 yd (45 m)/1.75 oz (50 g): color #3352

NEEDLES

Size 13 (9 mm) circular needle or size needed to obtain gauge, at least 24" (61 cm) long

Size 15 (10 mm) circular needle or size needed to obtain gauge, at least 24" (61 cm) long

GAUGE

9½ stitches = 4" (10 cm) in garter stitch

Drop-Dead Gorgeous

STITCHES DROPPED ON PURPOSE

A dropped stitch usually strikes fear into the heart of a knitter. But in this case, stitches are dropped intentionally to create a lacy design element. You won't drop the stitches until the very end of your knitting and the entire shawl is knit in stockinette stitch, so this is a great take-along project. This shawl must be cast on using the long tail method; otherwise the bottom edge won't hold together correctly when the stitches are dropped. Also, if you need to change yarns for any reason, make sure to do so at the side (selvage). Do not change yarns in the middle of a row, because this could be where a stitch will be dropped.

The finishing touch on this shawl is adding fringe to the spaces created by the dropped stitches. Instead of knotting the fringe into a loop, decorative beads hold it in place. Choose beads with a particularly large opening.

KNIT TIPS

You will notice that the edges of this shawl roll toward the wrong side. This is because the shawl is knit in stockinette stitch—knit one row then purl one row. If a knitted item has more knit stitches than purl stitches on either side, it will roll toward the purl side.

YARN

 Lightweight rayon bouclé
yarn: 525 yd (480 m)
Shown: Blue Heron Yarns
Beaded Rayon; 100% rayon; 525 yd
(483 m)/8 oz (226 g): 1 skein color
Deep Copper

Medium-weight ribbon ⅜" (9 mm)
wide: 95 yd (87 m)
*Shown: Fiesta Yarns Gelato Ribbon;
100% rayon; 262 yd (241 m)/3 oz (85
g): 1 skein color #3137, Rain Forest*

NEEDLES AND NOTIONS

Size 6 (4 mm) needles or size
needed to obtain gauge

Blunt-end yarn needle

Safety pins

16 large beads, with large opening

Floss threader, optional

Ribbon crimps

Small pliers for attaching crimps on
beaded fringe

GAUGE

22 stitches = 4" (10 cm) in stockinette
stitch, measured before the stitches
are dropped

FINISHED SIZE

15½" × 54 (39 × 137 cm), not including fringe

SHAWL

Cast on 71 stitches using long-tail cast-on
method (pages 106-107).

Row 1: Knit each stitch to end of row.

Row 2: Purl each stitch to end of row.

Repeat rows 1 and 2 until shawl is about 54"
(137 cm) long, saving about 3 yd (2.7 m) for
binding off.

Bind off, dropping every 8th stitch. Follow the
detailed directions in Knitting Class, page 92.

FINISHING

Using the blunt-end yarn needle, weave in all
ends. Lightly steam-block using a steam iron
set on wool and never allowing the iron to get
any closer than 3" (7.5 cm) to the scarf.

FRINGE

1. Test how many strands of ribbon will fit
   through the hole in a bead. I used 7 strands
   of yarn for each fringe, so 14 strands had to
   fit through the hole. Nudge them through
   with the blunt end of a yarn needle or use a
   floss threader to pull them through.

2. Multiply the number of strands in each fringe
   by 16 (eight fringes for each end of the
   shawl). Cut this many pieces of ribbon, each
   15" (38 cm) long.

3. Bundle all the strands of one fringe together
   and pull them through the space made by
   one of the the dropped stitches on one short
   side of the shawl. Pull one end of the strands
   through the bead. Then work the opposite
   ends through.

4. Even up all the ends and slide the bead up
   to within 1" (2.5 cm) of the shawl edge.

5. Wrap a ribbon crimp around the strands just
   below the bead and pinch it closed.

6. Repeat steps 3 to 5 for the remaining fringe
   bundles.

Lightweight Linen

Drop-stitch striping also looks beautiful when knit from a simple yet elegant yarn. You'll fall in love with the drape and style of this shawl, knit from a rayon and linen blend yarn. Knit this variation using the same amount of yarn, same number of stitches, and same needle size. Finish by wet blocking (page 111). Leave the edges unadorned for a more casual look or dress it up with ribbon fringe after you block it.

YARN

 Lightweight rayon/linen blend yarn
Shown: Madil Yarns Sahara; 70% rayon, 30% linen; 120 yd (110 m)/1.75 oz (50 g); color #66

NEEDLES

Size 6 (4 mm) needles or size needed to obtain gauge

GAUGE

22 stitches = 4" (10 cm) in stockinette stitch, measured before the stitches are dropped

KNITTING CLASS

Drop Stitch

It's time to drop those stitches.

Have faith!

1. With the right side facing you, count and mark every 8th stitch on your needle using a safety pin (close the pin around the front leg of the stitch but leave the stitch on the needle). Begin and end with seven stitches.

2. Bind off in the usual way until you get to the 8th stitch (the one you've marked). Remove the safety pin and drop this stitch off your left needle. Remember, don't panic—you're doing this on purpose. The dropped stitch will begin to leave a "run" down your knitting, just like your panty hose.

1

2

3. Notice that a gap has been created where you dropped the stitch. You need to "bridge the gap" by creating some new stitches to bind off. Next to the single stitch on your right hand, make a counterclockwise loop around your left thumb with the working yarn. Stick the needle into the bottom of this loop, taking it off your thumb and putting it onto the right needle. Pull the working yarn gently to snug the loop on the needle.

4. Now you have two stitches on the right needle and you can bind off one stitch.

5. Repeat steps 3 and 4 two more times, making a loop around your thumb, placing it on the needle, and then binding it off.

6. Repeat steps 2 to 5 across the row. Finish by binding off the last seven stitches on your needle.

7. Work the "runs" from the dropped stitches all the way down to the cast-on row by gently tugging from side to side next to each dropped stitch.

3

Be Happy

GARTER STITCH TRIANGLE

Would you even think of having a bad day if you were wearing this shawl? The bright color always makes me smile and the wonderful soft cotton makes me think of spring no matter when I wear it. The technique is really easy to learn. After making your first triangle shawl, you can experiment with an array of different needle sizes and yarns.

The concept for making a triangular shawl is really simple—start with three stitches and increase by one stitch at the beginning of each row. You'll have to knit side-to-side on a circular needle because you will quickly have too many stitches to fit on a shorter single-point needle.

KNIT TIPS

Do you know the Five Foot Rule? With arms outstretched, fingertip to fingertip on the average woman is about five feet. I usually allow 1 to 1¼" (2.5 to 3.2 cm) of yarn per stitch for the tail when I'm casting on with medium-weight yarn. If my scarf has 120 stitches, that's 120 inches (305 cm) or 10 feet (3 m). Using the Five Foot Rule, that's two fingertip-to-fingertip stretches with a little extra thrown in for insurance.

YARN

Super bulky bouclé yarn:
300 yd (274 m)
Shown: Blue Heron Yarns
Cotton/Rayon Boucle; *75% cotton,
25% rayon; 150 yd (138 m)/7.4 oz
(210 g): 2 hanks color Daffodil*

NEEDLES AND NOTIONS

Size 13 (9 mm) circular needle or
size needed to obtain gauge, at least
24" (61 cm) long

Size 15 (10 mm) needle or size
needed to obtain gauge, optional for
binding off

Blunt-end yarn needle

GAUGE

10 stitches and 18 rows = 4" (10 cm)
in garter stitch

FINISHED SIZE

22" x 44" (56 × 112 cm)

SHAWL

Cast on 3 stitches.

Row 1: Knit 1, knit into the front and back of
the next stitch (increase 1), knit 1.

Row 2: Knit 1, increase 1, knit each stitch to
end of row.

Repeat row 2 until the yarn is almost gone,
leaving 6 to 7 yd (5.5 to 6 m) to bind off. Bind
off loosely. If you tend to bind off tightly, then
use the larger needle for the bind-off row.

FINISHING

Using the blunt-end yarn needle, weave in all
ends. That's it—you're done. No blocking is
required. Talk about happy!

Multi-fiber Yarn

With polka dots, mohair, and merino wool, this shawl is just as cute as it is soft. And all three fun features are rolled into one multi-fiber yarn.

As you experiment with different yarns for this triangle shawl, let the label on the yarn be your guide for which size needle to use. Because I want my shawl to drape, I usually choose needles one or two sizes larger than the manufacturer's recommendation. To make a shawl the same size, you'll need 350 to 400 yards (319 to 364 m) of yarn. Or just follow the same pattern until your shawl reaches the dimensions you want.

YARN

 Medium-weight multi-fiber yarn
Shown: Classic Elite Yarns Minnie; 23% kid mohair, 16% merino, 38% nylon, 23% polyester; 120 yd (110 m)/1.75 oz (50 g): color #6093

NEEDLES

Size 8 (5 mm) circular needle or size needed to obtain gauge, at least 24" (61 cm) long

GAUGE

12 stitches and 20 rows = 4" (10 cm) in garter stitch

Mashed Potatoes

CHENILLE AND FUR YARNS KNITTED TOGETHER

At the yarn shop, we call this the "mashed potatoes shawl" because it's so gloriously soft, you just want to cuddle up in it, nestle into the sofa, and eat mashed potatoes. The softness of this shawl is only surpassed by its beauty, the result of combining two hand-dyed yarns of similar colors but different textures. The body of the shawl is made by knitting with both yarns held together. I used shiny ribbon yarn for a knitted edge, but you could choose to use the yarn for ribbon fringe.

KNIT TIPS

When you give a knitted item as a gift, don't underestimate how important it is to the recipient. Believe me, they won't see the funny stitch on row 34 or the uneven edge on your bind off. What they will see is the time you took to be a friend. Be sure to include the label from your yarn (keep a copy for yourself) so they will know how to care for the item.

YARN

 Super bulky weight chenille yarn (A): 300 yd (274 m)
Shown: Colinette Isis; 100% rayon; 109 yd (100 m)/3.5 oz (100 g): 3 hanks color #101, Monet

 Medium-weight fur yarn (B): 300 yd (274 m)
Shown: Colinette Silky Chic; 100% nylon; 223 yd (205 m)/3.5 oz (100 g): 2 hanks color #101, Monet

 Super bulky weight ribbon yarn (C): 30 yd (27 m)
Shown: Colinette Firecracker; 100% nylon; 77 yd (71 m)/3.5 oz (100 g): 1 hank color #101, Monet

NEEDLES AND NOTIONS

Size 13 (9 mm) circular needle or size needed to obtain gauge, at least 24" (61 cm) long

Size 17 (12.75 mm) circular needle or size needed to obtain gauge, at least 24" (61 cm) long

Blunt-end yarn needle

GAUGE

8 stitches and 15 rows = 4" (10 cm) in garter stitch

FINISHED SIZE

27" x 54" (68.5 x 137 m)

SHAWL

With yarn A and yarn B held together, cast on 3 stitches using the smaller needle.

Row 1: Knit 1, knit into the front and back of the next stitch, knit 1—4 stitches.

Row 2: Knit 1, knit into the front and back of the next stitch, knit to the end of the row.

Repeat row 2, increasing by 1 stitch every row, until you have 108 stitches. The length from the point where you cast on to just below your needle should be about 27" (69 cm). Bind off very loosely. If you tend to bind off tightly, then use the larger needle for the bind-off row.

RIBBON EDGING

Start by attaching the edging to the two diagonal sides of the shawl using the larger needle. The needle will be long enough to work down one side, turn the corner at the point, and then work up the other side. Don't get too crazy about picking up the exact number of stitches. Your goal is to pick up about two stitches per inch (2.5 cm).

Row 1: With yarn C, pick up and knit approximately 75 stitches on each side—150 stitches.

Row 2: Bind off.

Now attach the edging to the long side.

Row 1: With yarn C, pick up and knit approx 110 stitches.

Row 2: Bind off.

FINISHING

Using the blunt-end yarn needle, weave in all ends. As you are doing this, close the little space between the ribbon edging on the long side and each of the short sides. It is not necessary to block this shawl.

Ribbon Knitted with Fur

This technique works just as well for a combination of ribbon and fur. The ribbon gives the shawl body, and the fur practically melts at your fingertips. Instead of knitting a border, use the ribbon by itself to make fringe. Knit this combination on larger needles, following the same directions. Bind off when your shawl has 150 to 160 stitches. You will need about 500 to 600 yards (455 to 546 m) of each yarn. Allow for more yardage if you are making a ribbon fringe.

YARN

 Super bulky weight ribbon yarn
Shown: Lion Brand Incredible; 100% nylon; 109 yd (100 m)/1.75 oz (50 g); color #202

 Bulky-weight fur yarn
Shown: Moda Dea Chichi; 100% nylon; 91 yd (84 m)/1.75 oz (50 g): color #9948

NEEDLES

Size 15 (10 mm) circular needle or size needed to obtain gauge, at least 24" (61 cm) long

GAUGE

11 stitches and 18 rows = 4" (10 cm) in garter stitch

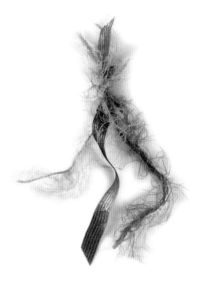

Hot Sauce

RIBBON KNITTED IN LACE STITCH

This sassy red shawl is the perfect complement to your little black dress. Knitted with a beautiful ribbon yarn, it has just a touch of metallic. The directions combine two knitting skills: knitting a triangle shape by increasing on every other row, and knitting in a simple lace pattern. This pattern can be just a bit complicated to learn, and it's intimidating to start right in on expensive ribbon. Use some plain yarn from your stash to learn and practice the pattern first. If you want a larger shawl, continue the pattern until you've reached the size you want.

KNIT TIPS

Knitting with ribbon is only difficult if you make it so. The ribbon doesn't need to lie flat for every stitch or align any particular way. As you knit, the ribbon might twist or fold over for a while. That's okay; it will just enhance the texture of your knitted fabric. Remember, knitting should be relaxing, not stressful.

YARN

 Bulky-weight ribbon yarn:
165 yd (166 m)
*Shown: Great Adirondack
Yarn ¼" (6 mm) Irisee Ribbon; 95%
rayon, 5% polyester; 100 yd (91 m)/
2.4 oz/(68 g): 2 hanks color Apple*

NEEDLES AND NOTIONS

Size 15 (10 mm) circular needle or
size needed to obtain gauge, at
least 24" (61 cm) long

Size 17 (12.75 mm) circular or
singlepoint needles or size needed
to obtain gauge

Blunt-end yarn needle

3 large-hole gold beads

Large-eye beading needle for
pulling yarn through beads

GAUGE

8 stitches and 16 rows = 4" (10 cm)
in lace stitch

FINISHED SIZE

17" × 39" (43 × 99 cm), not including
tassels

SHAWL

Using the smaller needle, cast on 4 stitches.

Row 1: Knit each stitch to end of row.

Row 2: Knit 1, yarn over, purl 2, yarn over,
knit 1—6 stitches.

Row 3: Knit 1, * yarn over, purl 2 together
*, repeat from * to * until last stitch, knit 1.

Row 4: Knit 1, yarn over, purl 1, * yarn
over, purl 2 together *, repeat from * to *
until 2 stitches remain, purl 1, yarn over,
knit 1.

Repeat rows 3 and 4 until the desired width,
leaving about 6 yd (5.5 m) for binding off.
Bind off very loosely using the larger needle.

You increase your stitch count only on the
even numbered rows. It's really helpful to
know which side you are on in case you
put your knitting down and can't remember. As you begin making your shawl, use
a safety pin to mark the side of your knitting with even numbered rows. Then if you
can't remember what side you are on, just
look for the pin.

FINISHING

Using the blunt-end yarn needle, weave in
all ends. You don't need to block this scarf.
If it seems a little stiff, mist it lightly with
water and allow the scarf to dry on a flat,
towel-covered surface.

TASSELS

1. Cut two pieces of yarn, each 36" (91.5
   cm) long. These will be the long tassels
   at the side points of the shawl.
2. Working one side at a time, thread one
   piece of yarn through the shawl point.
   Even up the ends and use the beading
   needle to pull the ends through the bead
   one at a time.
3. To make the tassel at the back, cut two
   pieces of yarn, each 12" (30.5 cm) long.
   Thread both pieces through the back
   point. Even up the yarn ends and then
   thread through the eye of the bead one at
   a time (you may need to use the large-
   eye beading needle).
4. Trim the ends of all the yarns to even up
   and remove frayed edges as necessary.

Larger Scale

Since this is such a quick project, you'll want to experiment with lots of different ribbon yarns. Just follow the basic pattern using needles that are at least one or two sizes larger than suggested on the yarn label. Stop knitting when you've reached the desired size or when you're about to run out of yarn—you'll need about 140 yards (127 m). Use the same technique to knit this shawl, but because this ribbon is wider and more textured, use a larger needle.

YARN

 Super bulky weight ribbon
Shown: Caron Pizazz; 100% nylon; 28 yd (26 m)/1.75 oz (50 g): color #785

NEEDLES

Size 17 (12.75 mm) circular needle or size needed to obtain gauge, at least 24" (61 cm) long

GAUGE

7 stitches and 12 rows = 4" (10 cm) in lace stitch

There are four basic knitting skills: casting on, knitting, purling, and binding off. It's that simple. More complicated pattern stitches are just different combinations of knit and purl. The directions in this book are very basic because that's all you need to complete the projects, but I encourage you to spend time learning other techniques from knitting reference books. Indeed, the second book you should buy (after this one) is a good reference book; several are made small enough to fit in your knitting bag.

CASTING ON

Casting on is the way the first stitches are put on your needle; think of it as the foundation row. Most new knitters feel that casting on is the most difficult skill to learn. Although it may seem awkward at first, it will quickly feel natural.

Slipknot

The first stitch of any cast-on row is the slipknot—you probably learned this knot as a kid. Here's another lesson:

1. Wrap the yarn counterclockwise around two fingers of your left hand (the ball of yarn is on your right, the tail of the yarn is on your left). Can you see that this makes a loop?

2. Reach under the loop with your right hand, grab the working yarn, and pull it through loop. Now you have a new loop in your right hand with a knot around the bottom. Put your needle through this loop and then pull the two strands of yarn at the bottom in opposite directions until the stitch is snug (not tight) on the needle. You've just made your first stitch.

Long-tail cast on

Look at the yarn under the slipknot. The short end is the tail; the end connected to your yarn ball is called the working yarn. If your pattern tells you to cast on 20 stitches, then the tail needs to be long enough for those 20 stitches. My rule of thumb is to allow 1" (2.5 cm) for each stitch, so your slipknot should be at least 20" (51 cm) from the beginning of the yarn.

1. Start with the slipknot on the needle and hold the needle in your right hand. Using your left hand, put your thumb and index finger between the tail and the working yarn. The tail should be around your thumb and the working yarn should be around your index finger. Use the other fingers of your left hand to hold both strands snugly against your palm. With your palm facing you, spread your thumb and index finger apart and pull back gently with the needle in your right so the strands of yarn are tight. The whole thing looks like a slingshot.

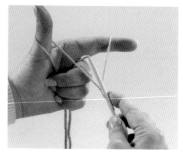

2. Insert the needle upward through the loop on your thumb.

3. Pivot the needle to the right and go over and then under the yarn on your index finger, thereby picking up a loop.

4. Now pull that new loop back down through the loop on your thumb just the way you came up.

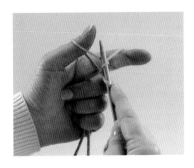

5. Let your thumb drop out of the loop and reinsert it through the tail and working yarn. Spread your fingers apart to pull the two strands at the bottom of the stitch gently so the stitch is snug (not tight) on the needle, next to the slip-knot. You've just made your second stitch.

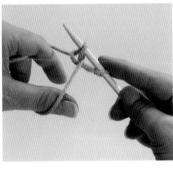

6. Spread apart your left thumb and index finger again into a slingshot. Repeat steps 2 to 5 until you have as many stitches as required by the pattern. Each loop on your needle represents one stitch.

KNITTING

Knitting stitches form flat vertical loops, or Vs, on the side of the fabric that faces you. The working yarn is held behind the needles.

1. Hold the needle with the cast-on stitches in your left hand. Hold the empty needle in your right hand with the tip pointing to the left. Working from front to back, insert the empty needle into the first stitch on the left needle, going through the loop just above the bump. The working yarn will be in back of both needles.

2. Hold the needles so they form an X (the right-hand needle will be in back). Wrap the working yarn around the right hand needle in a counterclockwise direction. The yarn will end up between the needles.

3. Holding the right-hand needle and the working yarn together, dip the needle down and toward you, drawing the working yarn through the first stitch on the left needle. The right needle will now be in front of the left needle with a new loop of yarn on it.

4. Slide the right needle upward and to the right, taking the newly formed stitch off the left needle (the original stitch will come with it). You've just completed a knit stitch.

5. Repeat steps 1 to 4 across the row for each subsequent stitch. You have completed one knit row. Notice that the right-hand needle is now the "full" needle. Transfer it to your left hand with the tip pointing to the right to begin a new row.

PURLING

Purl stitches form pebbly, horizontal bars, or bumps, on the side of the fabric that faces you. The working yarn is held in front of the needles. Purling is the alter ego of knitting—the wrong side of purling looks like knitting, just as the wrong side of knitting looks like purling.

1. Hold the needle with the stitches in your left hand. Hold the empty needle in your right hand with the tip pointing to the left. Working from back to front, insert the empty needle into the first stitch on the left needle, going through the loop just above the bump. The working yarn will be in front of both needles.

2. Hold the needles so they form an X (the right-hand needle will be in front). Wrap the yarn in a counterclockwise loop around the right needle.

3. Holding the right-hand needle and the working yarn together, dip the needle down and toward the back, drawing the working yarn through the first stitch on the left needle. The right needle will now be in back of the left needle with a new loop of yarn on it.

4. Slide the right needle upward and to the right, taking the newly formed stitch off the left needle (the original stitch will come with it). You've just completed a purl stitch.

5. Repeat steps 1 to 4 across the row for each subsequent stitch. You have completed one

purl row. Notice that the right-hand needle is now the "full" needle. Transfer it to your left hand with the tip pointing to the right to begin a new row.

Switching between knit and purl

When you are knitting, the yarn is always at the back of the work. When you are purling, the yarn is always at the front of the work. If you switch between knit and purl, such as for seed-stitch or rib-stitch patterns, it is necessary to bring the yarn back and forth between the needles. In seed stitch, for example, you would knit one stitch, bring the yarn between the needles to the front, purl one stitch, take the yarn between the needles to the back, knit one stitch, and so on. Remember, the yarn should go between the needles when moving back and forth, not over or around them!

BINDING OFF

Binding off is often called casting off, and it is how the final row of knitting is taken off the needles. Binding off creates a finished edge that will not unravel.

1. Knit two stitches onto the right-hand needle in the usual way. Now you're going to play leapfrog. Using the left needle, lift up the stitch that is farthest away from the tip (the first stitch you knit) and pass it over the second stitch and off the tip of the needle. Get it?

Leapfrog! When you are first learning to bind off, you might find it easier to lift up the stitch with your fingers.

2. Knit another stitch onto the right needle. (If you're going to play leapfrog, you have to go get another friend.) Once again, pass the first stitch over the second stitch. Continue in this manner until there are no longer any stitches on the left needle and just one stitch on the right needle.

3. Cut the yarn and leave a tail that is at least 8" (20.5 cm) long. Remove the needle from the last stitch and pull the loop gently with your fingers to make it a bit larger. Reach through the loop with your thumb and forefinger, grab the tail, and pull it back through the stitch. Continue pulling until the loop shrinks and is snug against the knitting.

Binding off in pattern

When you've made an item using an overall pattern of knit and purl, such as a ribbing, it should be bound off in the same pattern unless otherwise stated (this is often referred to as keeping to the pattern). When binding off, work two stitches at a time as always but knit or purl the stitches in the same pattern used to make the scarf.

Bind off loosely

It is essential that you bind off loosely, especially on the long edge of a shawl. An edge that is cast off too tightly is not only unsightly but the stitches can be weakened and will break with wear. If you have a tendency to cast off too tightly, just use a larger needle for the cast-off row. You might need to use a needle two or even three times larger than the needle used to knit the garment. If you've used a circular needle for your project, it is not necessary to use another circular needle for the cast off, since you only need the bigger needle for working two stitches at a time.

CIRCULAR NEEDLE
Some of the scarves and shawls in this book have too many stitches to fit on straight needles, even if they are 14" (35.5 cm) long. The solution is to knit back and forth on a circular needle. Think of the circular needle as two regular (single-point) needles that have been tied together with a string. The first challenge will be casting on. Hold the needle in your right hand as usual. As you cast on more and more stitches, they will slide off the needle and onto the cable (the string). When you've finished casting on, transfer the needle to your left hand with the needle tip pointing to the right. With your right hand, pick up the other end of the needle. Just ignore the cable and start knitting with your right hand as always. Again, because the row is so long, as you knit across, the stitches will move off the needle and onto the cable. When you've finished the row, all the stitches will have been transferred to the right side of the needle. Now, switch again—put the needle that's in your right hand into your left hand with the tip pointing to the right. Pick up the empty side of the needle and start the next row.

JOINING NEW YARN
As you knit a scarf requiring more than one ball of yarn, you will need to join a new ball of yarn. The most important thing to remember is that you must leave a tail at least 8" (20.5 cm) long that can be woven in when you finish knitting.

If your yarn isn't too thick, you can actually tie the new yarn to the tail of the old yarn at the beginning of a new row. Use the new yarn to tie half of a square knot around the tail and then slide the knot until it rests firmly against the edge of your knitting. Don't pull the bump through the stitch—leave it resting along the edge. You most certainly should use this technique with very slippery yarn.

When knitting with really bulky yarn, simply stop knitting with the old ball of yarn at the end of one row and start the new ball on the next row. Some knitters worry about this method, since it looks like it might unravel your knitting. You can tie half of a square knot to hold the two in place

until you finish but untie the knot before weaving in the ends so you don't add a bump.

WEAVING IN ENDS
After you finish knitting, there will be several tails left over from the cast on and bind off. There might also be tails along the edge where you joined a new ball of yarn. You can't just cut them off, or your hard work will begin to fall apart. You must weave the tail invisibly into the knitting so that it is secure, and then you can cut off any excess. Thread the tail onto a blunt-end yarn needle and weave it in and out of the knitting for about 3" (7.5 cm) along the side of the scarf. Then, weave the tail back in the opposite direction, still along the side of the scarf, for about 1" (2.5 cm).

INCREASES
An increase simply means adding a stitch to your knitting, thus making it wider. This book uses two types of increases: yarnovers and "knit into the front and back of a stitch." Sometimes an increase is paired with a decrease to create a decorative effect. In this case the overall stitch count will not change.

Yarnover
Before starting a new stitch, wrap the yarn over the right needle, creating an extra loop that is subsequently worked on the next row. A yarnover

is very distinctive because it leaves a hole in your knitting. Depending on whether you are knitting or purling the yarnover is different.

Knit: Bring the yarn forward and then lay it over the right needle in a counterclockwise direction, ending behind the two needles. Knit the next stitch. Notice that the yarn has made an extra loop on the needle.

Purl: Keeping the yarn in front, wrap it counterclockwise around the right needle. Purl the next stitch. Notice that the yarn has made an extra loop on the needle.

Knit into the Front and Back

This increase is sometimes called a bar increase because a visible, horizontal bar is formed on the right side of the work. This increase requires the stitch in which it's being worked to do double duty.

1. Knit a stitch in the usual way but don't take it off the needle.

2. Pivot the right needle around to the back of the left needle and insert it into the

back of the same stitch you just worked. Wrap the yarn around the right needle and pull a loop through the back-side of the stitch.

3. Slip the worked stitch off the left needle. You now have two loops on your right needle.

DECREASES

Occasionally a pattern will call for a decrease. This just means knitting or purling two stitches together as if they are one. This decrease can either be worked on a knit side row or a purl side row.

Knit: Insert the right needle into the next two stitches on the left needle. Work from the front to the back as usual, and knit two stitches at the same time. Wrap the yarn around the right needle, pull it through both loops, and slide the old stitches off the left needle. You have just decreased by one stitch.

Purl: Insert the right needle into the front loops of the next two stitches on the left needle. Wrap the yarn around the right needle, push it through to the back of both loops, and slide the two

stitches off the left needle. You have just decreased by one stitch.

PICK UP AND KNIT STITCHES

Sometimes you need to add an extra row of stitches to an item after it has been bound off or along the sides. In this book, this technique is used to add a ruffle to the bottom of a scarf; on a sweater it might be used to add a button band after the sweater has been knit. In most books you will see the wording just the way I've used it, but it seems confusing at first. You aren't actually knitting the stitch as you are picking it up. Rather, you are simply picking up the stitches as if you were knitting and leaving them on the needle. Stitches are picked up with the right side of the work facing you and using a separate ball of yarn.

1. Starting at the right corner, insert the needle from the front to the back going under two strands along the edge.

2. Wrap the yarn around the needle as if you were knitting and pull the loop through to the front. You have just picked up one stitch. Continue in this manner until you have picked

up the number of stitches specified by the pattern.

REPEATS IN PATTERNS

Often in knitting directions, you need to repeat certain groups of stitches within a row. In knitting patterns, asterisks are used to designate the beginning and end of a pattern repeat, like brackets. Repeat the instructions between the asterisks for the designated number of times or until you're told to do something else. For example, imagine you are making a seed stitch scarf. The instruction reads as follows: "* Knit 1, purl 1 *, repeat from * to * until 1 stitch remains, end with knit 1." In this case, you repeat * knit one stitch, purl one stitch * to the last stitch and end with knit one stitch.

BLOCKING

Blocking is one of the last things you do to your scarf or shawl before you wear it. It smoothes out the fabric, evens the edges, and enhances the drape. The process is done with either steam or water depending on the fabric content of the yarn. The project directions will specify which technique to use; often no blocking is required or even desired.

The first thing you need is a big enough space to lay your scarf flat. A towel or two placed on a padded carpet or on top of a bed works well (beware of Fido and Fluffy). I can often get away with just using my ironing board if I'm willing to do the blocking in stages. You may need to use pins to anchor the scarf to the towels or ironing board during the blocking process. Pins can help even up wavy edges or adjust for some width inconsistency.

Steam block

Hold the steam iron about 1" (2.5 cm) above the item and allow the steam to penetrate. In stages, set the iron aside and, using your hands, smooth out the fabric and make sure the width is consistent. Also, pay careful attention to the edges, making sure that they are straight and even.

Wet block

Lay the item on a towel and dampen it lightly using the fine spray from a misting bottle. Gently pat the scarf, allowing the moisture to penetrate. Pay particular attention to the selvages (long edges), making sure that they are straight and lie flat. Also, be sure that the overall width is consistent from end to end. Allow the scarf to dry completely before wearing.

FRINGE

Whether the fringe is simple or complex, it is a beautiful finish to the edge of a scarf or shawl and it's very simple to create.

1. Cut the fringe to twice the desired length plus 1" (2.5 cm). The fringe will be doubled, so keep this in mind when planning the length and number of pieces to cut.

2. Fold the fringe in half. Insert a crochet hook through the work and through the fold on the fringe. Pull the fold through so that about half of the length is on the wrong side, forming a large loop.

3. Reach through the loop and pinch the cut ends, pulling them back through the loop. Gently pull the ends down until the loop tightens.

YARN LABELS AND THE MEANING OF GAUGE

If you learn early in your knitting career to read a yarn label, you'll have much greater confidence as a knitter, and yarn shop owners will love and respect you. The first and most important information to look for is the yarn weight and gauge.

Patterns specify the weight of the yarn by using terms such as bulky, medium, light, with a corresponding symbol. Those terms and symbols are standardized classifications that are being adopted by designers, publishers, and manufacturers worldwide. The symbols are often used on yarn labels and they are incorporated in this book. First a word of caution: the term "weight" is misleading, since 99 percent of all yarn balls *weigh* the same—1.75 ounces (50 grams). Weight really refers to the *thickness* of the yarn. So, a "heavy" yarn, classified as super bulky, is thicker and therefore has less yardage in a 1.75 ounce (50 gram) ball than a "light" yarn, such as a fine baby yarn.

Yarn weight and gauge

Gauge refers to the number of stitches (horizontal) and rows (vertical) measured over 1" (2.54 cm) of knitting. Into 1" (2.54 cm) of knitting, you can fit more stitches of a fine yarn than a bulky yarn. Yarn labels include a square that represents the recommended gauge for that yarn when knit in a 4" (10 cm) square of stockinette stitch. Look for two numbers adjacent to the square. The number on the bottom indicates stitches and the number along the side indicates rows.

Choosing the right needle size

Another vital piece of information on the yarn label is the recommended needle size for that yarn. Remember that needles are sized according to the diameter of the shaft. The heavier the yarn, the bigger the needle needs to be. Fine (thin) yarn might be knit using a size 3 (3.25 mm) needle, while bulky (thick) yarn might require a size 11 (8 mm) needle. The needle size recommended on the label is the one that, when used by an average knitter, will produce the gauge (stitches per inch) shown on the label.

Use the needle size as a recommendation only; it's just a starting point. The average knitter would probably use that needle, but who says you're average? I'm not. I'm a very loose knitter. I usually use a needle that's two sizes smaller than recommended. If I didn't adjust the size to accommodate

my style, then my stitches would always be too big and my knitting would look sloppy. I take this into consideration when I design and write; I don't specify the needle size I used, but the size an average knitter would use.

How to make a gauge swatch

Every pattern will tell you what weight yarn to use, what size needle to use, and what the gauge should be. If you want your scarf to be the same size as the sample, then you must knit it at the same gauge. To ensure that you will get the same gauge, you must make a gauge swatch. Knitters hate making gauge swatches. They've just purchased beautiful, new yarn and they want to start knitting right now! Nevertheless, you will save yourself lots of disappointment if you take the time to make a swatch.

Begin the swatch by using the recommended needle and casting on the same number of stitches as indicated by the gauge in the pattern. For instance, if the gauge is 16 stitches = 4" (10 cm), then cast on 16 stitches. Begin knitting in the stitch specified next to the swatch. Knit in the pattern for several inches; don't try to measure the swatch after just a few rows (you knitters who try to do this know who I'm talking about). Measure your swatch from side to side, or parallel with the needle. If the swatch is 4" (10 cm) wide, then you are using the correct needle. If it is smaller than 4" (10 cm), then you need to use a larger needle; if it is larger than 4" (10 cm), then you need to

use a smaller needle. Don't try to change your personal style as a knitter (tight or loose); just change your needle size.

Yarn label hieroglyphics

In addition to gauge and suggested needle size, there's other vital information on the yarn label. Some is easy to understand, such as fiber content, weight, and length. You should also find the color number and/or name and the dye lot (batch). Finally, there's a bunch of symbols (they look like hieroglyphics) that tell you how to take care of the yarn. Here's a translation:

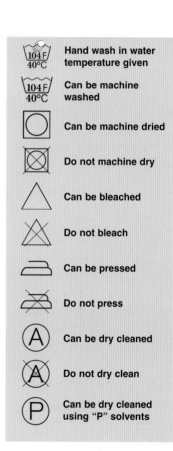

104F 40°C (hand)	Hand wash in water temperature given
104F 40°C	Can be machine washed
◯	Can be machine dried
⊠	Do not machine dry
△	Can be bleached
⊠	Do not bleach
iron	Can be pressed
iron crossed	Do not press
Ⓐ	Can be dry cleaned
Ⓐ crossed	Do not dry clean
Ⓟ	Can be dry cleaned using "P" solvents